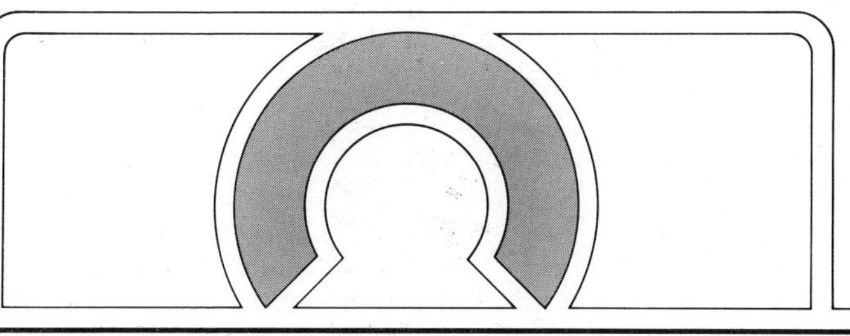

STUDENT'S TRANSCRIPT OF GREGG SHORTHAND FOR COLLEGES TRANSCRIPTION

LOUIS A. LESLIE
Coauthor, Gregg Shorthand, Series 90

CHARLES E. ZOUBEK
Coauthor, Gregg Shorthand, Series 90

A. JAMES LEMASTER
Editor in Chief, Gregg Shorthand Publications

KAY MENDENHALL
Instructor, Department of Business Education,
Mountain View High School, Orem, Utah

LORRINE B. SKAFF
Professor of Business,
Southern Oregon State College, Ashland

Gregg Division
McGraw-Hill Book Company

New York / Atlanta / Dallas / St. Louis / San Francisco
Auckland / Bogotá / Guatemala / Hamburg / Johannesburg / Lisbon
London / Madrid / Mexico / Montreal / New Delhi / Panama / Paris
San Juan / São Paulo / Singapore / Sydney / Tokyo / Toronto

Student's Transcript of Gregg Shorthand for Colleges, Transcription, Series 90

2 3 4 5 6 7 8 9 0 SESE 8 9 8 7 6 5 4 3 2 1

ISBN 0-07-037761-8

Explanation to Users of This Booklet

This booklet contains the transcript to the shorthand material in the Reading and Writing Practice exercises of *Gregg Shorthand for Colleges, Transcription, Series 90*. The number preceding each exercise corresponds to the shorthand exercise number in the text. This transcript will serve two desirable purposes:

1 It will enable the students to look up the word or phrase represented by any outline about which they are in doubt. They will thus be able to cover the Reading and Writing Practice exercises more quickly and with a minimum of discouragement.

2 Because the key material is counted, the students will be able to obtain extra dictation practice outside of class.

The Publishers

PART
CHAPTERS 1-8
Lessons 1-40

Transcript of Shorthand

(The material is counted in groups of 20 standard words, or 28 syllables, for convenience in timing the reading or dictation.)

CHAPTER 1

LESSON 1

3 Dear Mr. Peterson: Your application for a position with our firm as director of our warehousing[1] department reached my desk this morning. The practical experience you have had in this field is very impressive,[2] Mr. Peterson.

I have contacted the references you listed on your résumé. Each of them provided[3] some valuable information on your ability to work effectively with others and to manage[4] efficiently a complex, demanding business such as ours.

My assistant manager, Ms. Smith, and I have discussed[5] your application in detail, and we agreed that we should set up an interview with you at your earliest[6] possible convenience. We would like you to arrange with our personnel secretary to come to our[7] offices sometime next week if it is possible. You should plan to be with us at least two or three hours.

We will[8] reimburse you at the time of the interview for all your travel and miscellaneous expenses. Sincerely[9] yours, [181]

4 Dear Miss Nelson: I recently read your advertisement in a popular trade magazine for a manager[1] of your personnel department. I would very much like to be considered an applicant for that position.[2]

The attached data sheet outlines my education, experience, and general background. The position in[3] your organization should give me an opportunity to move into an area of management where[4] my educational training could be utilized profitably.

Your advertisement noted that an applicant[5] must be willing to work in any one of your branch offices throughout the eastern part of the country. I[6] would accept a position with your firm anywhere in the continental United States.

I will be happy[7] to meet with you at your convenience to discuss my qualifications in greater detail, Miss Nelson. My address[8] and telephone number appear at the top of this letter. You may reach me at my home after business hours.[9] Yours very truly, [184]

5 Dear Mr. Miles: Thank you very much for the opportunity of interviewing last week for a position[1] in your sales department. Your capable staff was certainly cordial, friendly, and informative. They did an[2] outstanding job of giving me a personal insight into the many facets of your outstanding, progressive[3] business.

It would be a good opportunity and a real challenge to be associated with your company.[4] I am certain that your firm will continue to occupy a prominent position in the field of[5] electronic equipment and supplies. It would be a pleasure to be part of that effort.

I have solicited[6] letters regarding my qualifications from several of my co-workers and my current supervisor.[7] Their comments may be valuable in helping you make a decision regarding my employment with your firm.

Your time,[8] energy, and effort on my behalf are sincerely appreciated. I hope to hear from you soon, Mr.[9] Miles. Sincerely yours, [184]

6 Dear Ms. Lee: Thank you for writing to us concerning sales openings in our organization.

During the past[1] two months we have been looking for capable, qualified people who would enjoy selling our products to schools in[2] two territories on the East Coast. Last week we interviewed two persons who met our requirements, and we hired them.[3]

We appreciate your interest in our organization, Ms. Lee. We regret that we cannot invite you to[4] join our staff at this time. Cordially yours, [87]

LESSON 2

3 Dear Mr. Bailey: Thank you for interviewing for the position of senior accountant with our firm. Our[1] personnel staff, the department head, and I have recently held several meetings to evaluate the candidates[2] for that opening. Each of the staff members who met with you was favorably impressed with your obvious[3] expertise in the accounting field.

We have, however, selected another individual to fill that[4] position. That person is one of our former employees and is well acquainted with our current accounting[5] procedures.

We would like to keep your application and personal data sheet in our active file for future[6] reconsideration, however. We will contact you immediately, Mr. Bailey, should another[7] opening occur.

It has been a pleasure to have the opportunity of becoming personally acquainted[8] with you. Sincerely yours, [165]

4 Dear Mr. Billings: I have been reviewing the applications and interview summaries of the several[1] people who applied for the vacant position in our credit department. I was indeed impressed with the[2] effective way you handled yourself during our interview. I believe, Mr. Billings, that our company may be[3] able to offer you a position of greater responsibility and higher compensation than the[4] one for which you applied.

It will be necessary, however, for you to make arrangements to complete an[5] additional battery of tests before we can come to a positive conclusion. Please call my secretary, Mr. Tate,[6] for additional details.

We are looking forward to hearing from you soon. Cordially yours, [138]

5 Dear Mr. Green: Thank you for your letter applying for a position with our firm. The brief description of your[1] educational training and your employment references indicates that you would be an excellent[2] secretarial candidate. We must, however, have additional information regarding your education,[3] your work experience, and your general background before we can pursue this matter.

Would you be good enough,[4] therefore, to prepare and send us a comprehensive, detailed résumé to help us evaluate your[5] qualifications.

We will be able to act on your employment request without delay if you will prepare and[6] send us this material as soon as possible. Cordially yours, [133]

6 Dear Ms. Adams: The salary, fringe benefits, and opportunity for advancement that your company offered[1] me as an executive trainee were quite generous. I am sorry, however, that I will be unable[2] to take a position with your firm. I have decided to accept a trainee position with another[3] company that offers exceptional potential for growth and higher earnings in the future.

I was very[4] much impressed with the caliber of people you employ. Your operations appear to be managed by competent,[5] capable executives who understand thoroughly the fundamentals of successful selling. I am[6] sure you will have no difficulty in finding outstanding people to fill any openings in your company.[7]

Thank you for your consideration. Sincerely yours, [150]

7 Dear Mr. Wilson: Several years ago you recommended Miss Mary Smith to us for a position in[1] our Mexico City office. Miss Smith has become so valuable an employee that we are promoting her[2] to the position of supervisor beginning the first of the year. This means, of course, that we will need someone[3] to replace her in her present position.

Do you know of anyone who would be interested in the job and[4] would like to live and work in Mexico City? The person we want is one who has the necessary skills and[5] can speak Spanish with some fluency.

Please call me collect if you know of such a person, Mr. Wilson. Sincerely[6] yours, [121]

LESSON 3

3 Dear Mr. Brown: You are probably aware that last month Robert Jones, our medical supplies representative[1] in your territory, was severely injured in an automobile accident. Mr. Jones is recuperating[2] and is undergoing extensive rehabilitation at a local physical therapy center.[3] His progress, however, is rather slow.

We want to continue to provide the services to which you are[4] entitled, of course. It is necessary, therefore, for us to assign another person to the territory[5] Mr. Jones has served. We have selected one of our outstanding salespeople, Miss Ann Baker, to fill that[6] vacancy.

Miss Baker has been a representative in Georgia for several years. She is an enthusiastic,[7] industrious person. She has a strong desire to serve her customers in the most helpful way possible.[8] On several occasions customers have expressed praise for her outstanding work.

Miss Baker will be contacting you[9] personally sometime before the end of the month. We hope you will arrange to take enough time to become well[10] acquainted with her when she calls. Sincerely yours, [209]

4 Fred Roberts: One of our finest drafting engineers, Barry Fox, left our firm several months ago to accept[1] a position in Detroit. We originally felt the void created by his leaving could be filled by our[2] existing staff. Now, however, it is rather obvious that we must hire someone to fill that vacancy.

Please[3] inform your staff to begin looking for an applicant for our drafting department. We need someone who has had[4] a number of years of experience and who is a dependable, creative person. We would, of course, like[5] to have someone who could begin work immediately.

We are prepared to pay whatever is necessary[6] to hire a qualified person. We have developed a rather large work backlog since Mr. Fox left.

Please keep me apprised[7] of your progress in this matter. John Foster [148]

5 George Farmer: I recently received the results of a job study by Max Phillips, our marketing supervisor.[1] His research indicates that the Providence area itself is now large enough to justify a sales[2] representative. Several retail outlets there are currently ordering our publications through the mail.

Would[3] you be interested in opening up that territory, George? Providence is a fine city in which to live.[4] Your family members are certain to enjoy the many advantages Providence has to offer.

We would[5] be willing to guarantee your current earnings during the first year in Providence while you establish your[6] clientele. We will, of course, pay all your moving expenses and cover any loss you may incur on the sale of[7] your present home.

Let me know immediately if you are interested in this new assignment. A. L. Franks [159]

6 Dear Mr. Jacobs: I just received a letter from one of our former employees, Miss Mary Green, telling me[1] that she is applying for the position as your secretary and asking permission to use my name as[2] a reference. I am quite happy to give her permission to do so.

Miss Green was my secretary for[3] several years. She is a good shorthand writer and an accurate transcriber. She also gets along well with people.[4]

I am confident that she will do an excellent job for you if you decide to hire her as your secretary,[5] Mr. Jacobs. Yours very truly, [108]

LESSON 4

3 Ladies and Gentlemen: For many years your state employment service has been helping people in Maryland.

We[1] serve as a clearinghouse for employers who are seeking qualified personnel to fill vacancies. We test,[2] evaluate, and place men and women in jobs for which they are best suited. Our record of achievement over the[3] years has been impressive.

We want young people entering the job market to be aware of our services. We[4] therefore sponsor talks and seminars in schools throughout the state. We hope you will let us know as soon as possible[5] if you would like one of our speakers to visit any of your classes during the coming year. We can present[6] a large variety of helpful lectures, demonstrations, and simulations designed to acquaint your students[7] with our broad range of services. Yours truly, [148]

4 Dear Mr. Church: I am pleased to provide the information you requested regarding our former employee,[1] Miss Alice Hawkins.

Miss Hawkins worked for us as a clothing designer for many years. She terminated her[2] employment several years ago because of ill health. We rehired her the following year. Our absentee records[3] show that she missed no more work after she returned than our average employees did despite her health problems.

Miss[4] Hawkins was certainly one of our most conscientious, dependable, and faithful workers. She enrolled in[5] several evening school courses to keep up with the changes in clothing fashions, trends, and designs. She was solely[6] responsible for the design of several articles of clothing that we marketed very successfully.[7] We were greatly disappointed, of course, when she decided to leave us last month to move to another part of[8] the country.

I am confident that you will be satisfied with her performance if you decide to hire her.[9] Sincerely yours, [182]

5 Dear Students: An interesting employment trend has developed in the last few years. There is now a greater[1] demand for qualified secretarial personnel than ever before. The need for people with[2] secretarial, clerical, and stenographic skills is increasing daily.

Most of you will shortly be seeking[3] employment. You should have no difficulty in securing an excellent position this year if you observe[4] just a few fundamental principles.

Make sure your business skills are well polished and ready to use. Know exactly[5] what kind of job you want. Keep your employment file current. This file should include a comprehensive sample letter[6] of application, a data sheet, and several personal and business references. You should practice[7] interviewing to make sure that you do things just right to impress those who will interview you.

Your observance of[8] these few

principles will ensure you success in finding a position that will meet your goals and expectations.[9] Sincerely yours, [183]

6 Dear Mr. Lee: Do you want to keep your staff at top efficiency even during rush periods? Do you want[1] to keep the work flowing smoothly even though many of your staff members may be on vacation? Then take advantage[2] of the competent temporary help in which we specialize.

Call us when you need secretaries, stenographers,[3] and typists. Call us when you need clerks, keypunch operators, and receptionists.

We will send you reliable,[4] capable people at rates that will be easy on your budget. We will, in addition, handle all payroll[5] details ourselves. At the end of the month you will receive one bill for all the services we provided.

Call[6] us the next time you find your work piling up because of vacations or other reasons. Yours very truly, [139]

LESSON 5

3 Dear Mrs. Green: Thank you for your interest in our company. We were pleased to spend Friday afternoon with you at[1] our office here in Spokane.

We have evaluated the aptitude tests you took, and I am pleased to inform[2] you that your scores were better than average in all categories.

I do, however, have a question regarding[3] your employment history as indicated on your personal data sheet. The period of time from[4] 1973 to 1975 was omitted from your employment record. This was likely[5] an oversight, but we need to have this information to complete our research.

We will process your application[6] immediately when we receive this additional information. Sincerely yours, [137]

4 Dear Mr. Strong: I will be visiting your college next week for the purpose of interviewing seniors for teaching[1] positions in our school district.

We have one of the largest school districts in the state, and we are anticipating[2] having several openings next year for business education graduates.

We have been assigned a[3] room in the college placement department, and we will begin our discussions with interested teaching prospects on[4] Monday morning. Please ask your students who might consider teaching in our district to have their names placed on our[5] interview roster. The staff in the placement department will have the personal file for[6] each candidate ready for our inspection before we do the actual interviewing.

Our district offers many outstanding benefits[7] to beginning teachers. We hope that several of your students will elect to talk with us about their teaching[8] careers. Sincerely yours, [165]

5 Mr. Frost: We informed you in February that our company failed to increase our sales during the past year.[1] Our common stock earnings were, in fact, the lowest in our history.

We are doing everything possible to[2] increase our sales, of course. In the meantime, however, we must cut our operating costs if we are to stay in[3] business. We have decided, therefore, to eliminate several positions in the office, and, unfortunately,[4] your job is one that will be discontinued.

We regret having to take this action. Many of those[5] affected have contributed greatly to our past success. We will keep you on the payroll for the entire month of[6] November, but you are free to terminate your employment immediately when you obtain another[7] position. Please call me if you have any questions. Betty Parsons [150]

6 To the Staff: We are planning to hold a retirement dinner for Mr. George Barnes, our chief controller, early next[1] month. Mr. Barnes, of course, is well known to all of us. He has been with us since we opened our doors many years ago.[2] We are proud of his numerous, distinctive achievements, and we would like each of you to share this evening with us[3] in honoring Mr. Barnes.

Your division head has been asked to contact each of you personally to make[4] reservations for this occasion. We hope you will be able to be with us. It should be an enjoyable,[5] memorable evening for everyone. Ann Moses [109]

7 Dear Ms. Gates: It is with sincere regret that I must submit my resignation as a correspondent with your[1] organization.

Several days ago my husband was appointed credit manager of his company,[2] and, consequently, we will have to move to Omaha. I would like to have my resignation take effect the[3] end of this month.

The years I worked under your supervision have been very enjoyable, challenging, and[4] rewarding. I will never forget you and the many other fine people with whom I have had the privilege of[5] working. Sincerely yours, [104]

CHAPTER 2

LESSON 6

3 To the Staff: For several years many of you have inquired about the possibility of our establishing[1] a program for making discount purchases. Last month our special services representative, Don Nelson,[2] completed the arrangements for just such a program. Our plan will enable you to purchase a wide variety[3] of goods and services at well below the existing retail prices, and you will build your savings account[4] balance as well.

Here is how the plan works. When you present your card to one of our participating merchants, you[5] receive a sizable discount on your purchase. In addition, a small percentage of the purchase price will be[6] credited to your account at any savings institution you choose.

We hope you will take advantage

of this service.[7] The program is explained in complete detail in the enclosed circular. Dorothy Marks [157]

4 Miss Phillips: When I received your letter explaining the circumstances surrounding the grievances of some of[1] our employees, I assigned the responsibility of checking into the matter to our personnel[2] manager, Don Davis. I have his report before me, and it explains quite clearly how the matter in question came[3] about.

We had no intention of violating the terms of our negotiated agreement with the union.[4] However, it appears that some of our decisions have been made without strictly adhering to the contract[5] guidelines.

I suggest that you set up a meeting with the employees and their representatives so that we can[6] reconcile this matter as soon as possible. You can schedule the meeting in one of the conference rooms if[7] you wish.

When you have made the necessary arrangements, please let me know. Bill Miller [155]

5 To the Staff: We are planning a special program for our next management conference in Reno, Nevada. We[1] have invited Betty Miller, who is a consultant with a major corporation, to present some of the[2] exciting, innovative ideas she has developed in the area of sales promotion.

Miss Miller is[3] one of the most effective, capable sales consultants on the lecture circuit today. She has the type of[4] personality to which everyone relates, and she has the capability of helping companies[5] dramatically increase their sales volume.

As soon as we have worked out the details for this conference, we will let you[6] know. We expect all department managers and sales personnel to attend what we hope to be the most[7] exhilarating and profitable training session of the year. T. J. Peterson [154]

6 Dear Employee: Enclosed is your new identification card. When you present your card, it will serve as your building[1] pass and as your identification for cashing checks.

The card is extremely valuable. Therefore, I hope[2] you will sign it immediately and keep it in a safe place.

Please get in touch immediately with our building[3] services department if your card should be lost, stolen, or misplaced. We will promptly issue you a replacement.[4] James R. Green [83]

7 Ms. Harper: Attached is a list of the people on your staff and an indication of the number of vacation[1] weeks each person is entitled to during the coming year. I am sending this information to you[2] earlier this year than in the past so that you will have more time for scheduling and planning.

When you have discussed[3] vacations with the members of your staff, please fill out the vacation form that is also attached and send it to me.[4] If it is possible, I hope you will be able to do this by the end of the month.

Do not hesitate to[5] get in touch with me or my assistant, Ms. Green, if you have any questions about our vacation policies.[6] A. J. Baker [123]

LESSON 7

3 Dear Mrs. Underwood: Mr. Larry Franklin has requested a transfer from our advertising department[1] to our billing department in our Los Angeles, California, office because of personal reasons. Larry[2] confided in me that he has not been happy in his present job due to a personality conflict[3] with the supervisor there.

I have recognized this problem for some time. As a precautionary measure, I[4] discussed the situation last month with both of the individuals involved. This action, which I thought would solve[5]the problem, has failed to alleviate the situation, however, and it is apparent that the conflict[6] is interfering with other employees throughout that division.

We decided by mutual agreement[7] that Mr. Franklin should be transferred to the billing department when an opportunity arises. He is[8] a valuable employee, and I am sure he will be able to perform satisfactorily in a new[9] position. Sincerely yours, [185]

4 Mr. Stockton: As you know, I have been in poor health for several years. My condition has gradually[1] deteriorated to the point that I am now unable to do my work satisfactorily. My doctors tell[2] me that I may be able to stay on the job another year, but it is improbable that I can work beyond[3] that point.

A few years ago our association here at Lexington Laboratories negotiated[4] an early retirement option for all employees. I believe it would be in my best interest and that of the[5] company if I were to take early retirement.

My physician is preparing a report that I will submit[6] to the retirement committee for their consideration. Your support in this matter will be greatly[7] appreciated. James Williams [145]

5 Dear Mr. Bates: Our corporation has become a leader in the field of personnel training here in Chicago[1], Illinois, because we have introduced new programs in literally hundreds of specialized fields. The members[2] of our staff have designed courses to fit almost every business and office need.

As you know, a progressive[3] company cannot survive today without utilizing the enormous capacity of electronic[4] data processing equipment. Consequently, we have developed a new course that will provide your employees[5] with the very latest information on new methods and innovations in data processing.

Our program[6] is described in detail in the enclosed circular. If you are interested, simply return the attached registration[7] form, and we will reserve a spot in this exciting workshop for you. Cordially yours, [157]

6 To the Staff: Our accounting supervisor, Ms. Mary James, has brought an important matter to my attention.[1] Our employees worked significantly more overtime this past year than they did the previous year. As a result,[2] our actual payroll expense was increased greatly.

Therefore, we have instructed all department supervisors[3] to reduce the amount of overtime work during the coming year. We know that you will understand the reasons[4] for this decision. Lee Madison [87]

7 Dear Miss Turner: How you express your ideas may have a profound effect on your life. We at Wilson College would[1] like to help you live a fuller, more effective life through better communication.

In our new communications[2] course you will learn how to get your ideas across to others. You will learn how to persuade and convince people.[3] You will command attention and respect if you can express your ideas clearly when you are at a major business[4] conference or at an informal meeting.

As you can see by the enclosed application form, our next class[5] will begin soon, and enrollment is limited. Enroll now and take the step that may not only enrich your life[6] but help you get ahead in business as well. Sincerely yours, [131]

LESSON 8

3 Dear Member: Several months ago we received a number of requests that our recreation association[1] in our Pittsburgh, Pennsylvania, office develop a program to give members the opportunity of[2] making discount purchases on a wide variety of consumer goods and services. We are pleased to inform[3] you that the work has been done and the program is ready to go.

Enclosed is your card with your serial number[4] imprinted on it. Merely present the card at any of the business establishments listed on the attached[5] brochure, and you will receive a substantial discount on your purchases.

We are exceedingly optimistic[6] about the program. Nevertheless, if you encounter any unusual difficulties, please be sure to[7] report them immediately to your association representative. Cordially yours, [157]

4 To All Employees: A few months ago we decided to provide an exercise facility in our[1] Miami, Florida, building. The facility, which is located in Room 15, can be used before and after[2] work and during the lunch hour. We believe this will satisfy a real need of our employees.

We have purchased[3] a wide variety of exercise equipment. In addition, showers and dressing rooms have been provided[4] for both men and women.

If you wish to use this facility, you will need to bring your own exercise clothes and[5] a towel. We have no provisions for storing them on our premises. Don Anderson [115]

5 Dear Ms. Phillips: A few weeks ago a government agency in Dallas, Texas, released some data that should[1] be of vital interest to you. Surprisingly, the demand for employees in the office occupations during[2] the next decade will exceed that of any other area. There will be thousands of new jobs during this[3] period. Unfortunately, many of them will go unfilled.

If industrial corporations are to avoid[4] the negative consequences of such a shortage of skilled labor, you must take positive action now. We[5] encourage you to become involved with business education programs in your local educational[6] institutions. This will give you an opportunity to encourage students to seek employment in the[7] secretarial, stenographic, and clerical fields.

Contact the vocational counselors in the schools near you for[8] information on how you can help. Cordially yours, [170]

6 To the Staff: Enclosed is a schedule of the classes we will be offering during the coming year in our main[1] office here in Portland, Oregon. Never before have we made such a large number and variety of classes[2] available to our employees. We hope each of you will be able to find at least one class in which you[3] are particularly interested.

We are offering several basic communications classes as well[4] as our usual excellent courses in finance and banking. Our courses in secretarial skills, which are[5] always filled to capacity, will again be offered this year.

If you plan to take a class, please ask your department[6] head soon for registration forms and other information. Plan now to add some real zest to your activities[7] this year by enrolling in one of our exciting, worthwhile classes. Helen Weeks [155]

7 Dear Ms. Grace: I sincerely appreciate the time you spent with me yesterday telling me about your company[1] here in Albany, New York. I was impressed by the outstanding character displayed by each of your executives.[2] It is easy to understand why your organization is acknowledged as one of the top industrial[3] firms in the world.

I realize, of course, that there are no openings at the present time. However, I hope[4] you will keep my application on file for future consideration. Yours very truly, [97]

LESSON 9

3 Dear Dr. Porter: I have been employed by the Smith Institute in Indianapolis, Indiana, for[1] several years. Because of the many learning opportunities that the institute offers, this time has been[2] an especially gratifying one for me.

I was contacted recently by a representative from[3] a firm in the import and export business in Providence, Rhode Island. The company offered me a temporary[4] position that would provide lucrative financial benefits for me and my family. To take[5] advantage of this opportunity, I am requesting a sabbatical leave for one calendar year beginning[6] in July. I have checked the provisions of our leave policy, and it appears that I meet all the necessary[7] requirements.

I hope you will make a decision as soon as possible so that I can make my plans well[8] ahead of the proposed date. Sincerely yours, [168]

4 To All Employees: In response to your many requests for information on the fringe benefits package[1] provided by your company, the research department has compiled statistical data in which each employee[2] should be vitally interested.

Many of you may be unfamiliar with the outstanding benefits we offer.[3] The total cost of our package is nearly a third of the actual amount paid in salary to our[4] employees. This is one of the highest ratios in our industry.

Our transportation allowance, which covers[5] all kinds of travel, is substantially higher than the average for our industry. Our health care program[6] provides what we think is the best health care possible.

We hope you can appreciate the concern your company[7]has for the welfare of each of its employees. We will be happy to respond to any questions you may have.[8] Mary King [162]

5 Mr. Mann: While reviewing our evaluation reports recently, I noted that your absenteeism[1] record is unusually high. Despite several reprimands by your department supervisor, you have[2] made no apparent change in your attendance pattern during the past several months.

Confidentially, we cannot[3] tolerate this situation indefinitely. Unless you make immediate and substantial improvement,[4] we will be forced to terminate your services.

We hope your future actions will preclude the necessity[5] for our taking such drastic measures. J.R. Kent [109]

6 Dear Mrs. Baldwin: Enclosed are the test results you requested regarding the mechanical aptitude and[1] interest inventory of one of your regular employees, Bill Williams.

While there appears to be some question[2] as to his interest in performing the intricate mechanical functions you require, in our opinion he[3] possesses the necessary aptitude and skills to be successful. In fact, he ranks well above average[4] in each of the tests we administered.

I hope this information will enable you to make a decision[5] concerning the transfer of Mr. Williams to your office in New Orleans, Louisiana. Sincerely yours,[6] [120]

7 To the Staff: America is the place that is made of dreams, and government savings bonds have been helping many[1] people make their dreams come true.

Government bonds mature in a short period of time. That means your dreams can come true[2] faster than ever before. How do you buy government bonds? Simply call the payroll department and tell them you[3] want to join our savings plan. You will receive a blank to fill out, and each month thereafter the amount you specify[4] will be deducted from your paycheck and invested in bonds.

Before you know it, you will have accumulated[5] enough to make your dream become a reality. A. S. James [113]

LESSON 10

3 To All Employees: The Adams Business College is sponsoring a training seminar on the latest developments[1] in electronic equipment next Saturday in our industrial arts building. We have invited[2] the training team from Electronics Manufacturers in South Bend, Indiana, to conduct the classes. They[3] will discuss topics ranging from the transmission capabilities of the latest CB radio equipment[4] to the growing potential of miniature transistors in television components.

We suggest that[5] your employees who want to become acquainted with the newest information in the electronics equipment[6] field register in our lobby the morning of the seminar. Cordially yours, [125]

4 To the Staff: As you know, we have been studying the possibility of modifying the present work schedule[1] to permit some of our employees to work ten hours a day for four days a week. Our home office in Chicago,[2] Illinois, has given us the authority to move ahead with our plans, and we want to initiate[3] the program next month.

We plan to introduce the change gradually, and we propose to begin with the transportation[4] department. Their workday will begin at 7 a.m. and end at 5:30 p.m. The lunch period[5] will be reduced to a half hour, which we feel sure will be ample time.

Some of you may object to becoming[6] involved with this change. If you want to transfer to another department, please inform your supervisor[7] immediately. We are confident, however, that the majority of you will be pleased with this new schedule. Doris[8] Johnson [162]

5 Ladies and Gentlemen: In two weeks the Baker Training Institute is sponsoring a tax information workshop[1] for any of your employees who want to become acquainted with the new provisions in the tax laws. The[2] instructor is Mr. Sam Hastings, who was formerly with the government tax service in Dayton, Ohio[3]. He will provide your accounting personnel with the general information they need to comply with all[4] pertinent changes in the tax laws.

At this time of the year, the subject of taxes is probably among your top[5] priorities. Therefore, we hope you will enroll some of your staff in our workshop. Complete the enrollment forms that[6] are enclosed and send them immediately with your registration fee. We will send additional details[7] immediately. Cordially yours, [146]

6 Mr. Gray: For the past year we have been having difficulty hiring people with the technical skills we require[1] in our factory. I was, therefore, very much interested in some correspondence I received recently[2] from the National Association of Employment Directors in Lincoln, Nebraska. It outlined the[3] advantages of securing personnel through private employment agencies.

Their selection methods, which have been[4] tried and tested through long years of experience, appear to be quite successful. The majority of their placements[5] stay on the job several years, which is a very good record.

I suggest that you call the employment[6] agencies in our area and get acquainted with their placement directors. We should certainly exhaust all[7] possibilities in securing the type of quality personnel we need. Jane Stacy [156]

7 Dear Dr. Smith: I am happy to learn that it will be convenient for you to have me visit Wilson College[1] next month. Mr. Ralph Jones, whose opinions I greatly respect, gave me such a glowing report of your electrical[2] engineering program that I felt I just had to see it in operation if it was at all possible.[3]

Thank you, Dr. Smith, for your offer to meet me at the Salt Lake City, Utah, airport and for your thoughtfulness[4] in making a hotel reservation for me.

Would it be possible for you and Mrs. Smith to have dinner[5] with me while I am in Salt Lake City? I would enjoy the opportunity to get to know you and your[6] wife better. Sincerely yours, [125]

8 Dear Mr. Davis: Thank you for your interest in applying for admission to our executive training program[1] and for sending us your data sheet.

I wish I could tell you that your application has been accepted, but[2] I cannot. Ordinarily, we have openings in your area, but we have no vacancies at this time.[3]

We are, however, placing your application and data sheet in our active files, which we frequently review.[4] When an opening occurs, we will get in touch with you. Very truly yours, [94]

9 Dear Mr. Mason: Are you having difficulty getting a start in the career field of your choice? If you are,[1] perhaps a typewriter could be your secret weapon.

Learning typing and shorthand, which are vital skills in modern[2] business offices, can make you more employable. These skills will help you to get your foot in the door and start your career[3] in your chosen field.

Where do you acquire these skills? The Wilson Business College has a special course for college[4] graduates like you. When you complete the course, we will help you to obtain a position in the field of your choice.[5]

Classes start next month. A complete schedule will shortly appear in your local newspaper. Yours truly, [118]

CHAPTER 3

LESSON 11

3 Dear Mr. Brandon: Assuring the

citizens of Springfield that their air will be free of pollution is not an[1] easy task. At its last session the state legislature empowered our agency with the responsibility[2] of supervising all activities affecting the air quality here and elsewhere in the state. The success[3] we obtain, of course, depends on organizations like yours.

The practice of burning old growth from agriculture[4] lands early in the year is one of our most grievous sources of air pollution. Unless conditions are right,[5] haze can linger for days over several square miles from the burning of just a few acres.

Our agency has[6] just issued an order banning this type of burning without first obtaining a special permit. Your cooperation[7] in this important program is vital if we are to keep our air clean and free of pollution. Cordially[8] yours, [161]

4 To All Distributors: As you know, we have had an unusually heavy demand during the past few months for[1] deliveries of regular, premium, and unleaded gasoline. Our refineries have been unable[2] to keep pace with the record sales we have experienced. Unfortunately, we will not be able to make full[3] deliveries to your station until after the first of the year.

You will be permitted to increase the[4] retail price of gasoline several cents per gallon. This should help lessen the impact of the revenue losses[5] your station is certain to sustain because of decreased sales.

We are very sorry about the situation,[6] but we trust you can make a satisfactory adjustment to this emergency and satisfy most of[7] your customers' demands. Will you please let us know if any serious problems develop. Sincerely yours, [159]

5 To All Store Managers: Beginning in October, we will discontinue our policy of remaining open[1] all night. We received a letter from a government agency suggesting that we scrutinize our marketing[2] practices and make changes that will save energy.

The agency specifically recommended that any[3] business remaining open all night do so only if the economic benefits clearly justify[4] it. Since our grocery chain adopted the policy of staying open all night, revenues have increased somewhat.[5] However, our expenses have increased substantially. Our after-tax income has not appreciably changed.[6]

Will you please post notices of the expiration date of our present hours in conspicuous places throughout[7] your store to make your customers aware of the impending change. Jill Smith [153]

6 Dear Senator Billings: If you can withstand a rather shattering experience some Sunday afternoon, I[1] invite you to go for a leisurely ride through the beautifully wooded hillside area near Medford. We are[2] sure that your concept of the beauty of the area will be significantly changed and your senses abused[3] by what you see and hear during your trip.

The use of motorcycles and other similar vehicles in the[4] area has created a serious problem there. The erosion of our hillside areas, the contamination[5] of our water supplies, and the noise are more than many of our residents are willing to tolerate.[6]

Would you be good enough to meet with a group of citizens sometime within the next few days to explore remedies[7] for this situation? We would like someone with your background to sponsor legislation that would give us the[8] power to deal with this problem. My secretary, Mr. James, will call sometime next week to set up a meeting[9] with our group. Cordially yours, [185]

LESSON 12

3 Dear Ms. Trent: Health and safety are not just the business of government; they are everyone's business. Our company[1] is concerned with keeping our streams, our rivers, and our air as pure as possible. Those of us who make our living[2] at Baker Enterprises breathe the same air and drink the same water that our neighbors do. The environment is[3] ours as well as theirs, and we want to protect it.

Without the jobs our company provides, however, hundreds of[4] us could not enjoy the privilege of living here. Your recent order requiring immediate compliance[5] with the newly enacted government regulations could jeopardize our ability to stay in business[6] in this state.

We hope you will meet with our engineers sometime before the end of the month to clarify some of[7] the provisions of the law. We believe that reasonable people who are willing to work together can solve[8] problems for the benefit of all. May we hear from you soon. Sincerely yours, [174]

4 Dear Bill: Your letter inquiring about the use of special fuels for aircraft arrived at a time when our company[1] is doing a considerable amount of testing of alternative power sources. One of our most[2] innovative, promising projects involves a research grant from the government to design an aircraft powered[3] by hydrogen.

This plane would be capable of carrying several hundred passengers for great distances.[4] It would have a capability of flying at much higher altitudes than current aircraft.

As a fuel,[5] hydrogen burns clean and causes virtually no pollution problems. However, it is a well-known fact that it is[6] rather expensive.

I have included some general specifications for the project on which we are working[7] for your information. Will you please call me if you need additional help. Sincerely yours, [157]

5 Dear Mrs. Stevens: In yesterday's mail we received your letter of application and your data sheet. We called[1] the references you listed, and they gave you a first-rate recommendation. Because your qualifications[2] far exceed those of other applicants, we are prepared to offer you the position of research director[3] for our organization.

As you know, our group has done a considerable amount of monitoring of[4] the changes in the biological composition of the area lakes caused by numerous environmental[5] factors. Our studies show that chemical levels have greatly diminished in fish species in all the lakes[6] as a result of government regulation.

Our work is exciting, and many challenges lie ahead. It[7] will not be easy, but we are optimistic that scientists like you will help us solve the important problems[8] that we face.

We are looking forward to your contribution to our organization. May we hear from you soon.[9] Sincerely yours, [183]

6 Dear Stockholder: All of us want clean air, and America's automobile manufacturers are working on[1] many ways to help cut automobile emissions that contribute to air pollution.

One device that automobile[2] manufacturers are using to control emissions is an electronic system that uses our[3] solid-state components. This system enables your car to ignite gasoline with greater precision than it[4] does with conventional systems. This will result in reduced emissions.

This is another illustration of[5] the steps your company is taking to help purify the air we breathe. Our creative designers and engineers[6] are working on many other interesting, exciting projects. You will learn about them in our next report[7] to stockholders. Cordially yours, [147]

LESSON 13

3 Dear Miss Thomas: I recently had the privilege of attending the Educators' Idea Fair. Your company's[1] demonstration of a model community school ecology course was one of the most ingenious I[2] have seen. Your approach to teaching this important, up-to-date subject to today's college students is truly unique.[3] It appears to be just the type of learning adventure we need here at our college.

I have discussed with our[4] administration the possibility of including this course in our program in the future, and I have[5] been given tentative approval. If you could send us a sample set of your materials before the end[6] of the month, we will review them and place our order as soon as possible.

Please bill us for the materials[7] at the time of shipment. Cordially yours, [147]

4 Dear Mr. Moore: The investigative subcommittee that you recently appointed just finished compiling[1] its findings on the radiation in our area.

As you will notice, the radiation levels in almost[2] every category substantially exceed the suggested safety standards that have been established by[3] the federal government. While the levels actually exceed the suggested standards, there is no immediate[4] threat to the residents of the area. Although the subsoil readings are not high enough to promote[5] evacuation of the area, they are naturally a cause of great concern to us.

The complete report, which[6] is in the hands of the printer, will be available in two or three weeks' time. We will send you several copies[7] as soon as we receive them. If we can be of further assistance, please let us know. Cordially yours, [158]

5 Dear Dr. Franks: We are pleased to announce that you have been appointed to head the energy research committee[1] in your area. Your credentials qualify you for this appointment, Dr. Franks. We know that the accomplishments[2] of your committee will make a vital contribution to our long-range program.

You should plan to assume an[3] active role with the committee before the end of the month. We will send one of our training teams to your office[4] to discuss the program with you in detail. This should give you all the background knowledge you will need.

We are happy[5] that such a well-qualified person has been selected to head this important committee, and we are looking[6] forward to working with you. Sincerely yours, [128]

6 Dear Residents: During the past few years, the subject of energy has been on our minds as well as yours. One of[1] our main concerns is that we may be facing the reality of gasoline rationing. If that time comes, it[2] will produce significant changes in everyone's life-style.

You can prepare yourself now for any possible[3] future gasoline rationing by starting to use the commuter railroad whenever you come to the city[4] to work or to shop. It is a well-known fact that if more of our residents used this mass transit system, our[5] diminishing fuel supplies would last much longer.

Begin today; do your part in conserving our nation's critically[6] short energy supply by riding your local commuter railroad. Cordially yours, [136]

7 Dear Mr. Lopez: As you are aware, there is at present an energy crisis that may result in a[1] possible shortage of oil. We believe, however, that we are well prepared to meet our customers' needs for the[2] immediate future.

Nevertheless, we urge you to support our government agencies' requests not to use fuel[3] unnecessarily. In a few days' time we will send you suggestions on how to keep your use of oil to a[4] minimum.

The officers and directors of our company wish to thank you for your continuing business[5] and to assure you that we are dedicated to doing everything we can to supply you with all the oil[6] you need at the lowest possible cost. Sincerely yours, [130]

LESSON 14

3 Mr. Fox: An article in a recent health publication pointed out some alarming statistics on the[1] causes of cancer. It cited the conclusions made several years ago that many types of cancer are caused[2] primarily by environmental factors. Recent studies support those conclusions.

Many people readily[3] assume that these factors are related only to air and water pollution. However, the fact is cancer[4] is caused by a variety of things. Many employees develop cancer because they are exposed to[5] cancer-causing agents on the job.

Because you are our company's safety director, I would like you to[6] supervise our efforts to isolate our employees from harmful, potentially dangerous chemical contaminants[7] in our factory. We must make a strong commitment to preserving the general health of all our people.[8]

At our next staff meeting, I would like you to present some of your ideas on the subject. Sandra Washington[9] [180]

4 Dear Mr. Larson: I have just reviewed the state government's regulations on the levels of atmospheric[1] pollution that may be tolerated near an industrial site. These regulations supersede the present[2] guidelines and call for compliance within a year.

We have been working on the problems associated with[3] emissions from our operations for several years. Our timetable calls for reconstruction projects that will reduce[4] emissions significantly over the next few years.

If we are forced to meet the standards before that time,[5] our cost analysts feel that our profit margin may be eliminated. It is questionable whether we[6] would be able to compete with newly constructed plants if we raise the prices of our products to compensate[7] for increased costs.

We want to stay in business; a compromise on these new regulations is necessary if[8] we are to do so. Will you please meet with us sometime soon to discuss this situation. Cordially yours, [178]

5 Dear Mrs. Yates: I received your interesting letter in yesterday morning's mail; I plan to include it in[1] one of my forthcoming newspaper columns.

Your question focuses on a pertinent topic of considerable[2] current interest. In my column I intend to point out that one of the most effective ways to save[3] energy is to leave the family car in the garage as often as possible and to walk to nearby[4] destinations. Walking has been shown to be effective, safe exercise for most people. If Americans would alter[5] their life-style to include more walking, they might be able to improve their health and save our nation's fuel at the[6] same time.

Thank you for submitting your excellent letter to our editors, Mrs. Yates. Cordially yours, [138]

6 Dear Mr. Carson: Thank you for the report you submitted concerning the control of pollution at the Brown[1] Manufacturing Company. The ecology committee met in special session today to consider[2] your recommendations; we voted unanimously to accept them.

I want to congratulate you, Mr.[3] Carson, on the work your company has done to help clear the air of smoke and to purify our rivers during[4] the past few years. If your company continues its fine work, we know that you will meet your goal of complete[5] elimination of pollution in your plant within the next few years. Very truly yours, [115]

7 Dear Mr. Best: The major objective of the Baker Corporation is to help companies such as yours to[1] reduce the impact of pollution control costs. We are cutting the cost of pollution control with new, improved[2] ways to purify water. We are the largest company devoted to wastewater treatment in the world.

To[3] help manufacturers improve the environment and reduce the cost of pollution control, we have prepared[4] a booklet that tells what you can do immediately. Send for your copy today; you will be glad you did.[5] Cordially yours, [102]

LESSON 15

3 Dear Ms. Henry: Next month Mr. Don Kelly will present a lecture on his organization's concerns over[1] the ecological damage occurring in our county. The time and date of his presentation will be announced[2] in next week's newspapers.

Mr. Kelly is one of the most widely respected lecturers on environmental[3] concerns in the country. He has written articles for several national publications. In[4] addition, he has an enviable record in promoting local action and legislation to curb blatant[5] environmental abuses.

The meeting will be free to the public. We hope you will plan to attend. Yours truly,[6] [120]

4 Dear Mrs. Sanders: Perhaps the most direct relationship in nature is that which exists between the number[1] of wild animals in a given area and their habitat. Heavy snow covers the land several months[2] a year in areas such as ours. Our various animals' feeding grounds are, therefore, severely limited.[3] The amount and quality of feed available during these months almost totally determine the number[4] of animals that can survive on a given range.

If your organization would like to make a significant,[5] positive contribution to wildlife here in the state, we suggest that you work with our division in[6] improving the quality and quantity of feed available for our deer herds.

Our big-game department head, Mr.[7] Milton Fraser, will be glad to meet with your group to help you draw up specific plans for your project. Please call[8] him to arrange a meeting. Sincerely yours, [168]

5 Dear Dr. Simms: Most people become quite concerned when the air pollution in their towns and cities becomes so bad[1] that they can smell and see the chemical impurities in the atmosphere. They have every right to be concerned;[2] this is, of course, a natural reaction. However, these same people do not realize that the air they breathe inside[3] many public buildings may be almost as bad as the air outside.

Without an effective filtration system,[4] air may become so bad in restaurants, offices, and other public buildings, it may jeopardize the[5] health of those with respiratory problems.

Our organization is sponsoring legislation to improve[6] the quality of air in all public buildings. Would your association endorse this measure? Will you please let[7] me know your organization's decision within the next week or so. We want to include your name on our list[8] of supporters. Cordially yours, [166]

6 Dear Sue: Would you be willing to work with me during the next few months in monitoring the air-pollution stations[1] we have set up throughout the valley? The state government has given our office a grant to gather badly[2] needed data. We will need someone to spend several hours each day collecting and recording information.[3]

If you are interested in this assignment, please contact me as soon as possible. We must hire someone soon to[4] provide the training necessary to ensure our operation's success. Cordially yours, [97]

7 Dear Mr. Gates: Many people talk about fighting pollution and conserving raw materials, but they[1] ordinarily do nothing about it. We at Wilson Company are actually doing something about it.[2]

Beginning in June, we will open a reclamation center for wastepaper at our main building in Cleveland,[3] Ohio. You can take your old newspapers and magazines to this center, where we will be glad to pay you a[4] nominal fee for them.

This is one of our company's efforts, Mr. Gates, to do something about the control[5] of pollution. It is a public service that we are happy to offer. Very truly yours, [117]

8 Dear Mr. James: In January we held a meeting in Bangor on pollution control. The sessions we sponsored[1] dealt with the impact of new air and water pollution control laws on manufacturing companies. Many[2] representatives from government, industry, and education were guest speakers at these meetings. These people[3] also answered many extremely important questions from members of the audience.

The meetings were[4] recorded and transcribed, and the transcript of the proceedings is now available to all people interested in[5] pollution control. If you would like a copy of this transcript, fill out the enclosed form and mail it to us.[6] Sincerely yours, [122]

9 Dear Mr. Lee: You can help avoid an energy crisis by driving a Parker motorcycle rather than[1] a car. On a Parker you can ride for many miles on a single gallon of gas.

While you save on gasoline,[2] you can really enjoy the excitement of the road. Riding a Parker is fun.

Let us show you our complete line[3] of Parker motorcycles. We have many handsome models. Just pick your favorite, and one of our representatives[4] will teach you in a matter of a few minutes' time how to handle it.

If you are worried about fuel[5] shortages, switch to a Parker motorcycle. Very truly yours, [113]

CHAPTER 4

LESSON 16

3 Dear Mr. James: The best reason to buy a Davis automobile isn't its price tag. The best reason isn't[1] its beautiful appearance. The best reason isn't even its high standard of performance.

Actually, there isn't[2] one best reason; there are literally hundreds of reasons why you should make your next car a Davis. The[3] Lexington Agency, your local Davis dealer, will be happy to tell you all about the new Davis. We are[4] located at 400 South Main Street here in Reno, and we are open from 10 a.m. until 9 p.m.[5] every day.

Come by today and order a new Davis; you will congratulate yourself for many years to come.[6] Sincerely yours, [123]

4 Dear Ms. Blair: Ten or twelve years ago, the cost of automobile insurance was a minor expense in operating[1] a car. Today, however, spiraling costs may make it difficult for you to buy the insurance you[2] need. Some people pay as much as $1,000 or more each year for insurance.

Notwithstanding the extensive[3] rise in insurance costs during recent years, the East Coast Insurance Company can still furnish a comprehensive[4] insurance package that all good drivers can easily afford. You see, Ms. Blair, we specialize in low-risk[5] insurance. We reward safe drivers with rates far below those of our competitors. Furthermore, we review[6] each policyholder's record every five years and allow additional rate decreases to those with unblemished[7] records.

Shouldn't you find out today if you qualify for this special insurance? Call on us at our main[8] office at 32 East 76 Street. We are open from nine to six daily, and we will gladly give[9] you further information. Cordially yours, [188]

5 Mrs. Agronski: A department of the federal government recently conducted an interesting, informative[1] poll on the use of passive restraints in automobiles. Surprisingly, over 75 percent of our[2] population favor equipping cars with passive restraints rather than with ordinary seat belts.

Furthermore,[3] the majority of those polled said they would sometimes take steps to disconnect automatic seat belts in their new cars.[4]

The device that enjoys the greatest acceptance is the air bag. More than half of those polled stated they would pay as[5] much as $1,000 for air bags in their next car.

Because the use of air bags appears to be inevitable,[6] our research department should pursue extensive development and testing of commercially acceptable[7] products in this area.

Will you please develop a short proposal to present to the board of[8] directors when we meet on Wednesday, February 21. Dan White [173]

6 Dear Miss George: If your present car doesn't have an eight-track tape player, we suggest that you look into the outstanding[1] features of a new Washington stereo system.

The Washington brings all the latest technology of[2] the electronics industry right into your car. A Washington stereo system can be connected[3] easily and inexpensively to the speaker system of your present radio. It can even be expanded[4] to include as many as four additional speakers.

The cost of a Washington is quite low, and we can[5] arrange for convenient financing. You can own a Washington stereo system for as little as 75[6] cents a day.

Stop in at your Washington dealer today at 773 Ninth Avenue. We are[7] open from nine in the morning until six in the evening. From February 1 to March 15, all[8] Washington products are being offered at a 20 percent discount. Sincerely yours, [175]

LESSON 17

3 Dear Mr. Lane: Thank you for your letter inquiring about personal property taxes on motor vehicles[1] in our state. Your interest in our taxing policies is understandable; we are sorry, of course, that you[2] feel the $176 tax on your new automobile is excessive.

We levy a[3] personal property tax on automobiles at the time they are registered. The amount of tax depends on[4] what is paid for the car and its declining book value thereafter.

We have developed a comprehensive,[5] up-to-date table on which we compute the tax on used cars. This table is based on the resale value of each model.[6] The table is available to the public for inspection.

In our opinion the policy is fair,[7] and we review it regularly. Our program has remained essentially unchanged since it was introduced and[8] passed on January 10, 1978, by the state legislature.

If you have further questions, please[9] let us know. Cordially yours, [185]

4 Dear Ms. Best: Most experts acknowledge that the two most important safety features of your car are your tires and your[1] brakes. They can often make a life-or-death difference during an emergency.

At International Tire[2] Company we specialize in tires that will provide not only riding comfort but also the peace of mind you deserve[3] while driving on today's busy highways.

Our best-selling products are steel-belted radial tires. They are[4] engineered to provide the smoothest, safest ride possible. They are tested on more than 1 million miles of city[5] streets, interstate turnpikes, and country roads throughout the nation.

Drive in to your International dealer today.[6] Our tires currently are selling at a discount of 12 percent while our present quantity lasts. Cordially yours,[7] [140]

5 Dear Customer: Most men and women want their automobiles to last for a long time. The staff and management of[1] the Eastern Motor Company, where you purchased your new car, also want your automobile to last for a long[2] time. The average cost of buying a new standard-size automobile and keeping it for three years is about[3] 28 cents per mile. If you can keep that same vehicle for three more years, the average cost per mile decreases to[4] less than 20 cents.

If all motorists would tune up their cars regularly, drive within the posted speed limits,[5] and change their car's oil frequently, many of them could count on 10,000 or 20,000 additional,[6] trouble-free miles.

Bring your new car to our auto maintenance center regularly. You will be saving yourself money[7] in the long run. Cordially yours, [147]

6 Dear Motorist: Most of us don't think much about the battery in our car except when it won't start. Unfortunately,[1] that can happen at the most inconvenient times.

If you would like to join the thousands of men and women[2] who will never have to worry about their car's battery again, we invite you to come in soon to your Johnson[3] Battery Center and have a Johnson battery installed in your car. The Johnson battery is[4] permanently sealed and never needs maintenance. It is guaranteed to start in all kinds of weather for as long[5] as you own your car. In addition, its price is far below what you usually expect to pay.

Come in today;[6] we can install your Johnson battery for as little as $35 while you wait. Cordially yours, [139]

7 Dear Ms. White: We are sorry to learn that you are dissatisfied with the service you received on the automobile[1] that you purchased from our dealer in Trenton, the International Motor Agency.

I am forwarding[2] a copy of your letter to our district office in Philadelphia, Pennsylvania, with the request that[3] they investigate the matter and take steps to see that you obtain the service to which you are entitled on[4] your new car.

You will be hearing from our district office in a few days, Ms. White. Cordially yours, [97]

LESSON 18

3 Dear Fred: Our automobile dealership needs a new service department manager immediately. If you[1] know someone who would like to work with one of the oldest, finest companies in this state, please let me know.

We had[2] the misfortune yesterday of losing Mr. Max Brown, our longtime service manager, to a larger firm in[3] the Southeast. Under Mr. Brown's leadership we had expanded our service business more than 50 percent in[4] the past five years.

Naturally, we need a man or

woman who knows all about cars and is willing to keep up with[5] the rapidly changing industry. The person should exhibit strong leadership characteristics and be able[6] to get along well with the 18 members of our service department.

Our salary for this position[7] is $20,000 per year plus liberal benefits.

If you have someone in mind, please contact me before[8] the 15th of April. Sincerely yours, [168]

4 Dear Mrs. Ross: A recent newspaper poll indicated that the vast majority of car owners believe[1] that repair costs are too high. At Madison Auto Center we have been trying to do something about that image.[2] As a result, our customers return time and again to have us repair their automobiles. Why? They feel[3] that our prices are fair and reasonable.

At Madison Auto Center we don't base our charges on a[4] suggested fee schedule as some other repair shops do. We give you an honest estimate of the time required to[5] do the job, the price of the parts needed, and our labor fee. If we miscalculate these charges, that is our[6] responsibility. We never charge more than 10 percent above our original estimate.

If these reasons for[7] doing business at Madison Auto Center appeal to you, stop in soon to get acquainted; we open each[8] morning at 8 o'clock. Cordially yours, [167]

5 Dear Ms. Best: The class on basic auto repairs in which you are interested will begin on Thursday, September[1] 9, at 7:30 p.m. It will be conducted in the high school auto shop at 21 East Main Street.[2] The class will be under the capable leadership of Mr. Roger Sweet, a local mechanic, and is designed[3] specifically for people who want to learn to repair their own cars.

Instruction will be given on replacing[4] points, plugs, and condensers. After completing this course, you should have the ability to do minor repair[5] work on your own car.

The fee for the course is $25 and is payable the first evening of the class.[6]

We hope you will become a member of this class, Ms. Best. Sincerely yours, [133]

6 Ladies and Gentlemen: Everyone chooses a car that suits his or her own special requirements. To some, speed and[1] performance are the most important characteristics in an automobile. Others like a luxurious,[2] comfortable car. Still others want a vehicle that is rugged and can travel in out-of-the-way places.[3]

No matter what your requirements are, we believe we can fit your exact needs in the sales department of Morris[4] Motors. We are the largest, most progressive automobile dealership in the state. Our showrooms are open from[5] 10 a.m. until 9 p.m. every day except Sunday.

We would like to have the opportunity of showing[6] you how we operate. If you will bring this letter to our showroom sometime next month, we will give you a free[7] demonstration ride in the new car of your choice and a coupon entitling you to 25 free gallons of[8] gasoline. Sincerely yours, [165]

LESSON 19

3 Dear Mrs. Charles: The typical American has generally assumed that it is more convenient and less[1] expensive to own a car than to lease one. In the past, that was probably true. Today, however, circumstances[2] have changed, and many experts agree that in the next decade it may be less expensive to lease a car than[3] to buy one.

The average full-size American car now costs $7,000 or more. At Western Leasing[4] you can drive the same car from our parking lot with a long-term lease for only a few dollars a day. Under the[5] circumstances, don't you think you should look into the possibility of leasing your next car?

Drop in to Western[6] Leasing today and let me or one of my capable assistants explain our program in detail. Cordially[7] yours, [141]

4 Dear Mrs. Turner: Thank you for your patronage over the years. You have returned to our organization time[1] and again to make your new car purchases, and we regard you as one of our special customers.

As you know,[2] among today's best new car buys are last year's models, which must be liquidated prior to the end of the current[3] model year. We have 200 of these cars on our lot at 203 Fifth Avenue, and we must sell them[4] to make way for next year's line.

These vehicles are presently available at savings of approximately[5] $1,000 per car. The actual price, of course, depends on the size of the automobile.

Under the[6] circumstances, why not drop in today and let us show you just how much you can save. Cordially yours, [138]

5 Dear Mr. Smith: Thank you for your recent correspondence concerning the cost and quality of the painting[1] services our organization, the Eastern Paint Shop, offers. Since you wrote to us a few weeks ago, we have hired[2] Mr. Don Trenton, who is considered one of the best painters in the eastern part of the country. His work is[3] in constant demand in the finer custom-painting shops.

Mr. Trenton's specialty is vans, and his work must be[4] seen to be fully appreciated. If circumstances permit, we suggest that you come in soon to discuss[5] your plans with him for a decorative paint job on your van.

Our new shop is located at 3725[6] East Baker Street and is open from 8 a.m. until 5 p.m. daily. Cordially yours, [137]

6 Dear Mr. Carter: When you test-drive one of our trucks at Trucks Unlimited, you will have an experience you[1] won't soon forget. People who buy trucks generally want them to perform well under any circumstances. Whether[2] they want to transport people, to travel along previously inaccessible mountain roads, or to pull[3] a trailer, they will find that our trucks meet every need.

We have constructed a driving area on a 12-acre[4] plot north of our State Street office. It has been developed to simulate virtually every kind of driving[5] condition you might encounter while using your truck. When you drive a vehicle off our lot, you know it will[6] perform up to your expectations and standards.

Drop in today for a demonstration drive at our unique driving[7] area at Trucks Unlimited. Yours truly, [150]

7 Dear Mr. Stern: The National Insurance Company encourages good driving. In fact, we offer a special[1] good-driver rate for those who have not been involved in an accident during the past year. This is our way of[2] thanking safe drivers for their fine driving records. Eight out of ten of our policyholders qualify.

Of course,[3] we are not the only insurance company that offers a good-driver rate. However, we also offer[4] instant claim service. We have more than 10,000 full-time claim adjusters available to help you on a moment's[5] notice.

When your present policy expires, come to us; you will be making a wise move. Yours very truly,[6] [120]

8 Dear Mr. Collins: Is your car ready for your vacation? Vacation travel subjects your car to some of the[1] most rigorous conditions possible. You don't want to have car trouble in some distant location.

Therefore, before[2] you set out on your next vacation, you will be smart to find out if your car is in shape to withstand many[3] miles of hard travel. We assure you that if you will let our mechanics check your car, it will be in top working[4] condition when they are through with it.

Bring in your car soon for a checkup. You will be taking a wise step to ensure[5] that it will not spoil your family's vacation. Very truly yours, [113]

LESSON 20

3 Dear Miss Collins: This is obviously the harshest time of the year on your car. Its exterior suffers rust[1] and corrosion; the interior becomes muddy and wet.

To give your car a clean, fresh appearance, we invite you[2] to visit King Auto Center as soon as possible. We will clean your car so thoroughly that you will think you[3] are sitting behind the wheel of a new automobile. In addition, we will inspect the brakes, the tires, and the[4] electrical system. We will provide you with a comprehensive report of the condition of your car.

Only[5] $25 will buy all these services when you visit King Auto Center. Do yourself and your car[6] a favor; drop in soon. Very truly yours, [128]

4 Dear Mr. Frank: We received notification yesterday morning of your recent automobile accident[1] in which you were issued a citation for speeding. You now have a total of 18 points on your[2] driving record. As you know, 20 points is the maximum allowed before your license is automatically[3] revoked. Obviously, this is a very serious matter.

The law states that you must come to the municipal[4] building within two weeks and take both the written and the actual driving examinations again.[5] We want to know that your driving knowledge and skill meet our current standards.

Please ask for me when you come, and I will[6] administer your tests myself. Yours truly, [128]

5 Dear Mr. Clyde: Most of the changes that occur in your family automobile are not easily[1] recognizable. In fact, the most revolutionary changes are in the electrical system of your car.[2]

Previously, the electrical systems found in cars were relatively simple. However, the demands for[3] better, more efficient electrical accessories have forced automobile manufacturers to adapt[4] the technology of the electronics industry to the requirements of today's automobiles.

The Modern[5] Electronics Company is a pioneer in this field. Most new cars made in America and throughout[6] the world use our components in their electrical systems.

The next time you buy a new car for yourself or a[7] member of your family, find out how it has been improved through electronics. Cordially yours, [157]

6 Dear Alice: Are you still interested in purchasing our automobile? We have decided to sell it ourselves[1] rather than trade it in on the new car we are planning to buy. The resale price of our car is $2,000,[2] but we are willing to sell it for approximately $1,800.

The car is in good condition.[3] The electrical system works perfectly, and the tires are practically new. It has been driven only[4] 34,000 miles.

If you would seriously like to make us an offer, please call us as soon as possible.[5] Cordially yours,

[103]

7 To the Staff: We are at the present time seriously negotiating with the Wilson Motor Company[1] to lease automobiles for our sales staff. If the plan is accepted, it will be some time before it will go into[2] effect, but we want all representatives who are now planning to order a new car to know about our[3] plans. In the future, all expenses connected with business travel will be paid by the company.

As soon as[4] full details about the leasing plan are available, I will write you again. Henry H. Smith

[97]

8 Dear Mr. George: When you are behind the wheel of a car, a lot of things can disturb you. Such things as sharp curves, bad[1] weather, and poor drivers in other vehicles all distract you.

Consequently, we build the Johnson car with[2] easy-to-reach controls near the steering column for headlights, turn signals, and windshield wipers. We build the Johnson car[3] with large, easy-to-read gauges and meters that tell you how your car is performing. We also build the Johnson[4] with comfortable seats that hold you firmly in place.

Aren't these good reasons why your next car should be a Johnson?[5] Sincerely yours, [103]

9 Dear Mr. Jones: When there's something seriously wrong with your car, the last thing in the world you want to do is wait[1] a week or ten days before it is repaired. You'll never have to wait very long at the Johnson Motor Company[2] to have your car repaired.

At our repair shop at 345 West 21 Street we have 24 work[3] stations staffed by highly trained, experienced mechanics who are ready to give your car the service it needs when[4] it needs it. Of course, we guarantee that the work on your car will be done right. Don't take our word for it; ask our[5] customers. They are our best advertisements.

Let us repair your car the next time it needs tuning up or servicing[6] in any way. If you bring it in before Friday, June 3, we will give your car a complete minor tune-up for[7] only $24.95. Cordially yours, [151]

CHAPTER 5

LESSON 21

3 Dear Mr. Washington: The yearly process of completing income tax forms according to government requirements[1] is obviously too complex for many people. Determining depreciation, capital gains, and[2] investment credits can become the kind of job that should be given to an accountant or income tax specialist.[3]

If, on the other hand, your situation is like that of millions of others, you probably feel you can[4] complete your tax return yourself with just a little help. Our booklet, *Your Income Tax Return*, will enable you[5] to fill out your own forms by following a simple step-by-step method. The booklet sells for only[6] $3.95, which, incidentally, is deductible on your tax return.

The booklet is available[7] at most newsstands. Pick one up soon; you will be glad you did. Cordially yours, [153]

4 Dear Ms. Johnson: Have you ever wondered how some people seem to make money without even trying? Have you[1] occasionally wished that you knew the secret of their success? Our experience convinces us that there is no[2] easy way to make money or to be successful. Success comes only by learning and applying definite[3] principles.

Over the years the research department at the Franklin Company has tried and tested hundreds of[4] ideas that relate to the accumulation of capital and to business success. These principles are[5] summarized in a book entitled *Success: Your Ultimate Goal*.

Send for a copy today. When it arrives, read a[6] few pages to measure the potential of its message in your life. If you are convinced it is worth the money[7] at that time, forward your check for $15 to us to cover the purchase price and shipping cost. If you are[8] not completely satisfied with the book, simply return it to us. Sincerely yours, [175]

5 Gentlemen: A few days ago one of your newspaper carriers left a complimentary copy of the[1] *Weekly Reporter* at my door. Although I had casually glanced at your paper in the past, I had never[2] seriously read it or considered subscribing. After all, I reasoned, I already receive two daily[3] newspapers. What could the *Weekly Reporter* contribute to my reading pleasure?

I did, however, take the[4] opportunity to read that copy of the *Weekly Reporter*, and I was extremely impressed and somewhat surprised[5] by its excellent quality. I believe the local news it carries on all facets of our community[6] life serves a real need.

Enclosed is my check for $10, the price of a subscription. Please begin delivering[7] my copy of the *Weekly Reporter* as soon as possible. Yours truly, [154]

6 Dear Miss Temple: Thank you for your subscription to our magazine, *The Business News*. Your first issue should arrive sometime[1] before the 15th of March. Your complimentary copy of our booklet, *Tomorrow's Business Forecast*, is[2] already in the mail and should arrive shortly.

We hope you enjoy the timely, informative articles in[3] *The Business News*; they are written specifically to help you keep up with the trends and developments most likely[4] to affect your management decisions in the months to come.

You may wish to have additional information[5] on topics covered in the magazine. If you do, you may submit a requisition, and we will prepare a[6] personalized report based on all pertinent, current research on the subject you select for only[7] $25.

We hope you derive the same benefit from *The Business News* that our thousands of other subscribers[8] do. Sincerely yours, [164]

7 Dear Ms. Green: In the December 10 issue of *Business World*, you published an interesting, informative article[1] on the use of small computers in the business office. I enjoyed the article, and I agree with your[2] conclusion that there is a place for this type of equipment in most offices.

I am the publisher of[3] several magazines in Europe, and I would greatly appreciate having your permission to translate and reprint[4] your article in French, German, and Spanish. May I have your permission to do so? I know, Ms. Green, that[5] it would be of considerable interest to our readers throughout the world. Very truly yours, [117]

LESSON 22

3 Dear Dr. Brown: The editorial board of the *National Forum* would like to invite you to be a[1] contributing writer to our next yearbook. Your name was suggested by a member of our staff who has read several[2] of your previous articles on history.

We need an article entitled "Education and Social[3] Change" for our next yearbook. As you know, we offer only a small sum for contributions to our publication,[4] but the *National Forum* does carry considerable prestige.

Our publication deadline for this issue[5] is Tuesday, June 1. The manuscript should not exceed 10,000 words.

Will you please let us know as soon as[6] possible if we can count on receiving the manuscript from you. Cordially yours, [134]

4 Dear Ms. Russell: Thank you for your inquiry on resource materials for your personal development class[1] at Danville College.

In my recent book, *Personal Grooming*, Chapter 9 is entitled "Skin Care" and is devoted[2] to a discussion on how to keep your skin looking its best. At the end of the chapter is a bibliography[3] that lists more than 50 references on the subject. I am sure you will be able to find answers to[4] your questions from this extensive resource list.

If I can be of further help, please let me know. Yours truly, [98]

5 Dear Mrs. Long: Thank you for your inquiry of February 12 about income tax deductions. We suggest[1] that you read Chapter 29 in the *Income Tax Guide*. The chapter entitled "Business Deductions" covers all[2] the rules for reporting various types of expenses involved in operating a business. The regulations[3] are quite specific on the amount of deductions allowed. You should refer to these guidelines in the future[4] when claiming business deductions.

If we can be of further help to you in the future, please let us know. Cordially[5] yours, [101]

6 Mr. Franks: In the last issue of *Ski World*, Mr. Ben Tracy wrote an interesting, timely article entitled[1] "Snow Vacations" in which he featured ten of the top ski resorts in the country. He mentioned that each of these[2] resorts has package vacation plans that include lodging, meals, and the use of recreational facilities.[3]

We have had more than 2,000 requests from people throughout the country asking for additional information[4] on these package vacation programs. I believe we should prepare a brochure in which information on these[5] plans could be provided in detail. The resorts should probably be willing to pay for this kind of advertising,[6] and it could benefit the circulation of our magazine.

Let me know your reaction to this proposal.[7] If you are interested, we should act while people are still making their vacation plans. Larry Day [158]

7 Dear Mr. Davis: Thank you for the time you spent with me discussing the possibility of your publishing[1] my manuscript entitled "The World of Work" that I mailed to you.

After carefully studying the terms of the[2] proposed contract, I have decided not to accept it. I feel that the terms you offered me would not yield a fair[3] return on my investment of time and money in the preparation of the manuscript. According to the[4] terms of your contract, you would have to sell at least 50,000 copies of the book before I would receive a[5] royalty of $2,000. I consider this an inadequate return. Therefore, I plan to offer[6] my manuscript to another publisher.

Please return my manuscript to me by express. Sincerely yours, [139]

8 Dear Mr. Gates: I am enclosing three copies of the latest issue of the *Financial Magazine* in which[1] your article entitled "The Investment Future" appears. Your article has created considerable[2] interest; we have already received more than 200 letters, telephone calls, and telegrams about it. This[3] is the type of response we like to receive. We will print some of the letters in the "Letters to the Editor"[4] column of a forthcoming issue.

If you would like to have copies of the letters so that you can personally[5] thank your admirers and answer your critics, we will be glad to send them to you. Cordially yours, [118]

LESSON 23

3 Dear Ms. Jackson: Our publishing company has just printed a trial copy of a new magazine called[1] *Family Finance*. We prepared this publication in response to requests from readers throughout the country. Before[2] we decide to begin regular publication, however, we need input from several people whose[3] opinions we respect.

Would you be good enough to critique our magazine on the following points:

1. The[4] practicality of the subject matter.
2. The ease with which it may be read.
3. The quality of the illustrations.[5]

Your assistance in this matter will be greatly appreciated, Ms. Jackson. Cordially yours, [118]

4 Dear Mrs. Johnson: Approximately four out of every five families in Wilmington subscribe to the *Daily*[1] *Tribune*. Recently an independent research group asked our subscribers what features of our newspaper they[2] liked best.

The following information gained from the survey may be of interest to you:

1. The *Tribune* contains[3] complete, comprehensive news from one of the country's leading wire services.
2. The editorial section[4] features several nationally syndicated writers.
3. The sports news provides detailed coverage of local[5] events.

If you are not a current subscriber, return the enclosed coupon for a three-month trial subscription[6] at 40 percent off our regular rate. Cordially yours, [132]

5 Dear Mr. Sanders: An article in a recent issue of *Financial Digest* identified the economic[1] goals that are important to the majority of

Americans. The three objectives most people would[2] like to achieve are:

1. Steady and secure employment.

2. Enough income to provide a reasonable standard[3] of living.

3. A sound retirement program.

These subjects and dozens of other topics that vitally affect[4] the lives of all of us appear regularly in the *Financial Digest*. Every article is carefully[5] selected to provide the kind of current information you should have before you make important economic[6] decisions.

Buy a copy today. If you are not completely satisfied after reading it thoroughly,[7] notify us. We will give you a three-month free subscription to any other magazine of your choice.[8] Sincerely yours, [162]

6 Dear Reader: We are sorry to inform you that we are planning to discontinue publishing the *National*[1] *Sports Reporter*. Our final issue will be published in October. This decision was made because of the[2] following reasons:

1. Increased publication costs
2. Small yearly increases in sales
3. A loss of advertiser[3] support
4. Increased competition

Unfortunately, we have operated at a loss for more than two years[4] while we attempted to improve our financial situation. Our board of directors concluded that the road[5] ahead appeared too gloomy to justify our continuing operation.

We thank you for your subscriptions to[6] the *National Sports Reporter* during the past several years. Readers like you have made our job easier during[7] these troubled times. Yours very truly, [147]

7 Dear Mr. Nash: Wouldn't you like to have all the latest business news spread out before you each morning on your breakfast[1] table? If you would, treat yourself to home delivery of the *Times*.

Each morning you will receive all the latest[2] news on mergers, interest rates, real estate transactions, and other subjects. At the beginning of each business[3] day, read the business and financial pages of the *Times*.

It is easy to start home delivery service of[4] the *Times*. All you have to do is fill out and mail the enclosed form. In a few days the *Times* will be arriving at[5] your door by 6 o'clock each morning. Yours truly, [109]

8 Dear Ms. Pulaski: If you read the January issue of *Management News*, you no doubt found some ads for[1] companies you would like to have more information about. All our advertisers want to tell you more about themselves[2] than they have room for in their regular ads. Therefore, we have made it possible for you to send for further[3] information at no cost by simply using the enclosed form.

Here is all you have to do:

1. Scan the names of[4] companies listed on the enclosed form.

2. Decide which companies you would like more information about and[5] place a check mark next to their names.

3. Write your name and address

at the bottom of the form.

4. Place the form in the[6] envelope that is enclosed and mail it.

When we receive the form, we will notify the companies involved.

This[7] is one of the many services that we are pleased to render to readers of *Management News*. Sincerely yours,[8] [160]

9 Dear Miss Torres: When you are buying or selling real estate, a broker can save you time and effort for the[1] following reasons:

1. Brokers know the market.
2. They know what properties are available.
3. They know who the[2] best prospects are.

It is smart to consult a broker when you buy or sell real estate. To find a reputable[3] broker in your area, check the listing in the *Daily Tribune*. The *Daily Tribune* carries more advertisements[4] of real estate brokers than any other paper in West Virginia. Very truly yours, [97]

LESSON 24

3 Dear Ms. Taylor: Ask yourself this question, "Is my job truly satisfying?" If you cannot answer yes, perhaps[1] you should be in some other area of work.

For a satisfying, enjoyable job, we suggest that you[2] look into the fascinating world of publishing. There are currently jobs for editors, designers, and artists.[3] Each of these jobs offers wonderful opportunities for advancement for the person who really wants to[4] get ahead.

If you would like to have more information about the field of publishing, write to us today; we[5] will be glad to hear from you. Sincerely yours, [108]

4 Dear Mrs. Golden: On January 15, 1950, the General Company published the first[1] edition of *World History*. Recently we printed our fourth edition of this major volume. The latest[2] edition includes a detailed summary of every major event that has occurred since the third edition was[3] printed.

We received an interesting letter a few days ago from Ms. Martha Jennings, a high school history[4] teacher in Detroit, Michigan. Ms. Jennings stated, "*World History* is the most popular reference book in our[5] library." She went on to explain how quickly her students grasp the significance of historical events[6] because of the interesting way the book is written.

If you are not presently using *World History*, we[7] suggest that you send for an examination copy today. Sincerely yours, [154]

5 Dear Mr. Jones: As you may know, Miss Mary Wilson has been working on an article entitled "Flowers of[1] the South," which is scheduled to be printed in the June 15 issue of *Flower Magazine*. It will be an[2] excellent article containing several illustrations in color.

To celebrate the publication of[3] Miss Wilson's first article in a major magazine, I am planning a small party in my home at 703[4] East 23 Street from 5 to 7 p.m. on June 18. To this party I am inviting a[5] few of

Miss Wilson's personal friends.

I hope that you will be able to attend the party to celebrate[6] publication of "Flowers of the South"; I know Miss Wilson would like you to be there. Sincerely yours, [137]

6 Dear Ms. Joyce: We have been looking for a qualified editor for the past several months. Mr. Mark Keith, one[1] of my business acquaintances, recently mentioned your name and suggested that I contact you in reference to[2] the opening. He said, "Ms. Joyce has the education, the desire, and the experience to be one of the[3] finest editors in the business."

If you are interested in working in one of the largest, best-known publishing[4] companies in the East, please write to me as soon as possible. If you prefer, you may call me at[5] 555-8062. I hope to hear from you soon. Very sincerely yours, [113]

7 Mr. Allen: Yesterday I met with Miss Gail Sweeney, the supervisor of our pressroom. She said, "Unless we[1] are able to obtain an adequate supply of the high-quality paper we use in our printed materials,[2] we may be out of business before the end of the year."

The paper we use has been purchased from a[3] supplier in California. Unfortunately, that company recently went out of business, and we have not[4] been able to find another supplier.

Will you please contact other major paper suppliers to see if you can[5] develop new sources. Because our present supply is dwindling rapidly, we must make other arrangements[6] immediately. Ralph Cook [125]

8 Gentlemen: As you know, you were kind enough to print in the September issue of *Publishing Review* a letter[1] appealing to book companies to contribute books to correctional institutions.

The response was heartening,[2] but it was mainly from small publishers. We hope that some of the larger publishers will also cooperate[3] with us. We would, therefore, be very grateful to you if you would print an appeal to the large publishing firms[4] of the country.

If you do print another appeal, please send us a copy of the issue in which it appears.[5] Sincerely yours, [103]

LESSON 25

3 Dear Ms. O'Leary: Thank you for sending us a copy of your manuscript, "Outdoor Survival Skills." We appreciate[1] your sending it to our publishing company for consideration. I am sorry we cannot[2] accept it for the following reasons:

1. We have two other current publications on this same subject.

2.[3] The market for this type of publication is currently at a low ebb.

3. In our opinion, the manuscript[4] is too long and detailed for the market for which it is intended.

The editor who examined your work[5] included the following statement in the evaluation: "This manuscript has outstanding potential. I[6] believe it would be wise for us to reconsider its publication at a later date. Unfortunately,[7] there is no market for it at this time."

If you would be interested in submitting it again in the future,[8] please let us know. Sincerely yours,

PS. Your manuscript is enclosed.
[173]

4 Dear Mr. Flynn: We are pleased to announce that Ms. Mary Johnson has become an assistant manager in the[1] advertising department of our newspaper.

Ms. Johnson has done an outstanding job for us in several[2] assignments during the past seven years. Ms. Johnson has truly earned this new position through her dependability,[3] efficiency, and initiative. One of our customers recently stated: "Ms. Johnson is one of[4] the most efficient people with whom I have worked. Whenever I need advice on an advertising project, I[5] call her."

When you wish to place a future order in the *Daily News*, you should contact Ms. Johnson personally;[6] we assure you that you will receive excellent service. Cordially yours,
[133]

5 Dear Mr. Garcia: Twenty years ago we published our first issue of the *Medford Register*. Our primary[1] objective back in those days was to produce a newspaper that appealed to as many people as possible.[2] We were able to hire a staff with the technical skills necessary to produce a first-class paper.

In[3] the first edition our editor stated: "It is our intention to provide the citizens of Medford with[4] the finest newspaper on the market. We will spare no effort to accomplish this goal." Although we sold only[5] 2,000 copies of our first issue, our daily circulation exceeded 17,000 copies by[6] the end of the year.

Today we are one of the South's largest newspapers, and our dedication to our original[7] principles is as strong as ever. To help you get acquainted with our outstanding publication, please[8] accept a month's subscription with our compliments. Cordially yours, [172]

6 Dear Customer: We received a letter recently from the mill that supplies most of our raw materials. We[1] thought you might be interested in part of its contents. The letter explained: "As a result of recent problems in[2] the lumber industry, our production costs have risen substantially. It is, therefore, necessary for us[3] to increase the prices on all paper by 15 percent effective July 1."

We regret that it is[4] necessary for us to pass this additional cost on to our subscribers, but we have no other recourse. We[5] are, therefore, increasing the monthly subscription rate of the *Lexington Star* by 25 cents.

We hope you[6] understand the need for this increase. You may be sure that we will continue to deliver to your door the most[7] informative, comprehensive newspaper possible. Sincerely yours, [153]

7 Dear Miss Myers: Thank you for submitting to us your manuscript entitled "Travel in India." Our travel[1] editor read it and had this comment to make: "This article is fine, but we already have ten travel[2] articles in our pending files. These will carry us for the rest of the year."

Instead of accepting your manuscript[3] and filing it away for future use, we are returning it to you with the suggestion that you offer it[4] to another publisher who may be able to use it in the near future.

Thank you for your thoughtfulness in[5] submitting your manuscript to us. Sincerely yours, [110]

8 Dear Ms. Wilson: Mr. Parks was good enough to invite me to the party on June 18 to celebrate the[1] publication of your book, *Plants of the West*. Nothing would have pleased me more than to have had the opportunity[2] to congratulate you personally.

However, the date of the party conflicts with our annual sales meeting[3] in San Francisco, California; consequently, I will have to miss the event.

When I return from San[4] Francisco, I will make it my first order of business to purchase a copy of *Plants of the West*, which I hope[5] you will be good enough to autograph for me. Sincerely yours, [112]

CHAPTER 6

LESSON 26

3 Dear Mr. Barber: Last October we commissioned the Electronic Research Corporation to study the[1] cost of the various telephone services we provide. On Wednesday, February 13, I met with their[2] representative, Miss Doris Quinn, to discuss their findings.

Their study indicates that the service we provide[3] to several small communities in our county is not paying for itself. To recover the expense we[4] incurred two years ago when we installed the electronic switching equipment in these communities, we will[5] have to increase our residential and commercial rates by 18 percent.

I will have the complete report[6] available at our next board meeting. Can I count on your support for this recommended increase? Sincerely yours,[7] [140]

4 Dear Miss Mason: If you would like to increase the profit potential of your business, we suggest that you advertise[1] your services in the business section of the *Los Angeles Telephone Directory*.

We know from[2] experience that most people in our locality who are looking for service such as yours look first in the business[3] section. They can find what they want quickly and easily.

The cost of this service is lower than you might think.[4] Why not pick up your phone right now and dial 555-2121. One of our friendly, helpful employees will[5] explain how easily and inexpensively you can get your message across to more than 4 million prospective[6] customers. In order to have your advertisement included in the spring edition of the directory,[7] we must have your order by Friday, November 10. Sincerely yours, [153]

5 Dear Mr. Allen: On Christmas Day, which is now almost three weeks ago, we began having problems with the[1] telephones in our home. We notified someone in your service department, and a crew was dispatched to repair the[2] damage the following Thursday.

Unfortunately, they were unable to pinpoint the trouble, but we were promised[3] that the problem would be located and that the phones would be repaired within a few days' time.

Here it is the[4]middle of January, and we are still without dependable telephone service. We are discovering[5] the hard way what an important device our telephone really is.

Will you please help us. Sincerely yours, [118]

6 Dear Mr. Best: One day last week it seemed that I was out of my office every few minutes taking care of business[1] somewhere else in the building. By the end of the day I was exhausted, and I had accomplished only a[2] small part of the day's important work.

As I reflected on our communications dilemma, I remembered[3] the brochure you left me describing your new National Office Communications System. Will you please arrange[4] for one of your representatives to call me after Thanksgiving to discuss this innovative device.[5]

I believe we might be able to use your system to good advantage in solving some of our communications[6] problems. Sincerely yours, [125]

7 Dear Mrs. Overmeyer: Last Monday we received a clarification from the Federal Communications[1] Commission on the question of recording telephone calls without the consent of both parties. They emphatically[2] told us that rulings by the federal government expressly forbid this action unless prior consent[3] is given.

We know it is important to companies like yours to have a record of some of your telephone[4] conversations. That is why we developed a new telephone recording device. This device will permit[5] you to record calls with just the touch of a switch. To comply with the law, the device automatically informs[6] the other party that the call is being taped.

This new device is just one of the many innovations which[7] have made Modern Electronic Equipment the nation's leader in electronic technology. Sincerely[8] yours, [161]

8 Dear Mrs. Dempsey: Last spring my office procedures class toured your fine new telephone office on Pine Road. It was[1] a memorable experience for us all. The students still recall how informative and interesting the[2] tour was.

Would it be possible to arrange for a similar tour sometime this fall for our current group of students?[3] We can schedule our transportation for any Thursday or Friday morning during the months of September,[4] October, or November.

Because we are required to make arrangements well in advance for any off-campus[5] excursions, we hope you will let us know soon if your schedule will permit our visit. Sincerely yours, [118]

LESSON 27

3 Dear Mr. Lake: Keeping up to date on subjects of current importance is essential to all of us in making[1] business decisions and in conversing intelligently with our colleagues. Gathering the large quantity[2] of information that we need would take several hours' time each week if our only sources were the numerous[3] periodicals currently available.

We recommend that you examine carefully the enclosed[4] complimentary copy of *News Brief*. This magazine summarizes the important events of the preceding[5] week. It provides insight into the implications these events could have on the course of American business.[6] The magazine is written for the person who needs a great deal of information but who has little time to[7] read.

News Brief will enable you to broaden your knowledge and to communicate with your employees, business[8] associates, and personal friends in a manner that will command their respect and attention. This weekly publication[9] sells for only $35 per year, a very small price to pay for keeping up with world events.[10] Just return the enclosed form along with your check, and we will start your regular subscription to *News Brief* beginning[11] with the October 1 issue. Sincerely yours, [230]

4 Dear Ms. Collins: Congratulations on your outstanding presentation at the Metropolitan Management[1] Training Conference in Chicago last week.

The program was exceptionally well organized, and the speakers[2] were all well prepared. I honestly felt, however, that your luncheon speech on improving office communications[3] was the highlight of the conference.

Would it be possible for you to furnish me with a copy of your[4] talk for distribution to my employees? I would like each person on my staff to be aware of the principles[5] of communications you discussed. Sincerely yours, [110]

5 Dear Mrs. Smith: No one can escape the necessity of communicating through writing. Whether we use[1] handwritten reports, typewritten letters, or other forms of written communications, others must rely on the[2] quality of our writing to interpret important messages.

The Johnson Institute is beginning a[3] new communications course on Tuesday, September 12. The course will consist of 20 lessons and will be taught[4] by Dr. Jane White, who has been such a successful teacher over the years.

Mr. James Garcia, one of Dr.[5] White's former students, acknowledged the value of our course in a recent letter. Mr. Garcia said: "I[6] received numerous comments and praise from my business associates on my writing ability after[7] studying at the Johnson Institute. I am now able to write clearly and effectively with less expense in[8] time and effort."

Perhaps some of your employees should enroll in our course. The enclosed circular explains our program[9] in detail. Sincerely yours, [186]

6 Dear Mr. Tate: We are currently preparing the annual report for our stockholders, and we would be pleased[1] if you would write a covering letter to accompany the statistical data.

The Suburban Telephone[2] Company has made rapid progress over the past few years. We now serve more than 10 million customers, and[3] our long-term growth rate still exceeds 10 percent per year.

Our capital investment last year was $14 million.[4] In spite of this investment, we are paying our common stockholders a $10 dividend, which is[5] another record for the company.

Our preliminary report is enclosed for your examination. Your[6] letter will be a welcome addition to the brochure we plan to circulate to our stockholders. Sincerely[7] yours, [141]

LESSON 28

3 Gentlemen: I read in our local newspaper, *The Times,* that the Reno Business School is offering a course in[1] speed reading that will begin Monday, February 12. Everyone in my company is interested in the[2] course, and we will probably have at least 20 who will actually take the course.

We think this class has excellent[3] potential in terms of helping every one of these employees to read more effectively. We do, however,[4] have the following questions:

1. What are the average reading speeds achieved by students who complete this course?
2. Is[5] this skill retained after a few weeks' time?
3. What is the total cost of the program?

May we hear from you sometime[6] soon. Sincerely yours, [124]

4 Dear Mr. Martin: On Friday evening, October 26, Western State College will be playing Lexington[1] College in football. We would like to broadcast that game to our home audience in Lexington. Consequently, we[2] must rent a telephone line for some time that evening.

Do you have a line available for our use? What is its[3] approximate cost? What regulations are involved in rendering this service?

We have not broadcast our games from[4] other cities in the past, but our fans' interest is growing rapidly. Therefore, we expect additional use[5] of your lines sometime in the future. Yours very truly, [110]

5 Dear Ms. Young: Would it be to your advantage to answer personally every one of the telephone calls that[1] come into your office 24 hours a day? It would be, of course. However, that is impossible.

You can,[2] however, respond to every one of your business telephone calls by providing general information[3] to your callers, taking messages, and returning calls at your convenience. How? You can do this by installing[4] a Jennings Telephone System. Jennings is the best friend a business executive could have. When you are out of[5] the office, your callers will be greeted by a friendly recorded voice. They can even leave a short message for[6] you if they wish. No potential customer will be forced to call another supplier because no one answers[7] your phone.

Please call our office sometime soon for a demonstration of our system. Sincerely yours, [157]

6 Dear Ms. Davis: The Edwards telephone amplification system is one of the most helpful communications[1] devices anyone has ever developed. With the flip of a switch, your callers' conversations are[2] amplified so that their voices can be easily heard 5, 10, or even 20 feet away. You don't have to hold[3] the phone in your hand, and you can have as many of your staff members involved in the conversation as you wish.[4] Yes, Ms. Davis, the possibilities of the Edwards system are almost unlimited.

Please complete the enclosed[5] card and return it in the enclosed self-addressed envelope. We will have one of our representatives arrange[6] to stop by sometime soon to spend some time with you demonstrating this new communications device. Sincerely[7] yours, [141]

7 Dear Mrs. Franklin: Everyone needs to brush up on his or her communications skills. Unfortunately, we[1] have never offered our employees any kind of special telephone training. Consequently, I believe our[2] business has suffered substantially from the general lack of skills many of us exhibit in the use of[3] our telephone equipment.

Does your company have a training representative who might be willing to set[4] up a program and spend some time with our staff in helping us use the telephone more effectively? We need advice[5] in transferring calls correctly, in using the hold button properly, and in developing better telephone[6] manners.

If you or your representative would call my office sometime soon, I would like to discuss the[7] possibility of instituting such a training program in our company. Sincerely yours, [157]

LESSON 29

1 *(As dictated)* Dear Ms. Taylor: Thank you very much for your kind letter of December 21. (Take out *kind*.) We were very happy to hear from you.

I am sorry, however, that the furniture you ordered from our company arrived in poor condition. I assure you completely (Delete *completely*.) that we will replace the shipment just as soon as possible. Unfortunately, we do not have in stock (Make that *we do not have all of the items you ordered in stock at the present time*.) However, we should have them in shortly. When we receive the shipment, we will write to you immediately. (Take out *immediately*.)

Thank you for your understanding, Ms. Taylor. Sincerely yours,

1 *(As it would be transcribed)* Dear Ms. Taylor: Thank you very much for your letter of December 21. We were very happy to hear[1] from you.

I am sorry, however, that the furniture you ordered from our company arrived in poor condition.[2] I assure you that we will replace the shipment just as soon as possible. Unfortunately, we do not[3] have all of the items you ordered in stock at the present time. However, we should have them in shortly. When we[4] receive the shipment, we will write to you.

Thank you for your understanding, Ms. Taylor. Sincerely yours, [98]

3 Dear Mr. Hastings: Have you ever missed an important call when you were out of the office? Have you ever lost[1] money because a customer could not locate you? If the answer is yes, we have the solution to your problem.[2] It is the Madison Paging System. Here is how it works.

When a customer calls your office, one of our[3] operators tunes in your frequency on an electronic device in our central office and then pushes[4] a button. This activates a small signal device you carry whenever you are away from your office. The[5] receiver makes an audible sound that alerts you to the fact that you have a message. You can then communicate[6] with the caller within minutes from the nearest telephone.

The Madison Paging System costs less than[7] $1 a day. Visit our showroom at 131 East Main Street here in Memphis, Tennessee, and ask for a[8] demonstration of our latest model. You will be making no mistake, Mr. Hastings. Cordially yours, [178]

4 Dear Mr. Kennedy: I would like to quote from a letter written to me by one of our telephone customers[1] who recently returned from a trip to a foreign country:

"A member of our tour group needed to call home[2] to check on a business matter. He was sent to the local government office to fill out an application[3] required by the government. He could not make his call until the next day. The following morning he went to the[4] local post office, which was the only place where long-distance calls could be made. It took more than three hours to get his[5] call placed, and the bill was $87."

The next time you make a long-distance call, notice the short time it[6] requires to place it and the low cost. We think you will agree that your local telephone service is one of the[7] best communications bargains in the world. Sincerely yours, [151]

5 Dear Mr. Barnes: No business executive can answer the telephone at all hours of the day and night. However,[1] much business is transacted after regular business hours. Unanswered phones could mean lost business.

If you are[2] not now using an answering service, we encourage you to begin at once. The Phillips Communication[3] Service is the largest answering service in Miami. We have five well-trained, experienced operators[4] on duty at all times. They will receive your calls when you are not in your office, screen them according to your[5] directions, and communicate directly with you when necessary.

The cost of our service is low, but the[6] convenience we provide can hardly be measured in terms of dollars and cents.

Pick up your phone now and call our answering[7] service. Let us give you an actual demonstration of how we will handle your calls for you. Sincerely[8] yours, [161]

6 Mr. O'Brien: The cost of our long-distance telephone calls to offices in the San Francisco, California,[1] area has averaged more than $340 during each of the past six months. This is an[2] important expense item in our budget. I believe it would be inadvisable to reduce the number[3] of calls we make to San Francisco; such action would jeopardize the large volume of business we do there.

Perhaps[4] the solution to the problem lies in leasing a long-distance line into the area. If we had had a[5] line there during these past six months, our telephone expense would have been considerably less, and we would have had[6] unlimited access to our customers.

With your permission, I will take immediate steps to lease a[7] long-distance line. June Stevens [144]

7 To the Staff: A problem in the use of our telephone system has been brought to my attention. Any employee[1] who picks up a telephone should check to make sure the line is clear. If a call has been put on hold, it is[2] automatically disconnected when someone picks up the telephone on that line and then hangs up.

Of course, it is[3] a matter of courtesy not to pick up a line that is being used by someone else. Your cooperation[4] in this matter will be greatly appreciated. Mary George [92]

8 To the Staff: As you know, we have worked long and hard to secure the recent large order from the Bennington Company.[1] That company had been purchasing their chemical supplies from an out-of-state distributor and had been[2] satisfied with the service they had been receiving.

After their initial order, I wrote them a simple thank-you[3] letter. Their response to that gesture was gratifying. Their purchasing agent said, "This is the first time any[4] company has gone to the trouble of writing us a thank-you letter."

Will you please make it a policy[5] in the future to write thank-you letters whenever an important order is received. If the Bennington[6] Company's reaction is typical, this one small idea may be an important factor in increasing our business[7] in the future. Dan Ford [145]

LESSON 30

3 Dear Mr. Newton: We would be happy to have you bring your business procedures class to our stock brokerage firm[1] at 460 Williams Avenue on Friday, April 14, at 9 a.m. We appreciate the[2] opportunity to demonstrate the role of electronic communication in the investment business.

I have[3] asked Mrs. Harrington, my secretary, to send you a few copies of *Avoiding Investment Mistakes,* one[4] of our publications that should be of interest to your students. If you will acquaint your students with the information[5] in this booklet, they will appreciate more fully the many functions of a modern stock brokerage[6] house.

We are looking forward to your visit. Cordially yours, [131]

4 Dear Mr. Gordon: The Southern Telephone Company always tries to keep up with the latest innovations[1] in communications equipment. When a new device is developed, we make it available to our[2] customers as soon as tests show that it is reliable, efficient, and dependable.

A few months ago we[3] started a program that will convert our present mechanical switching equipment to electronic switching.[4] Although this conversion process will cost more than $1 million, we actually anticipate a modest[5] decrease in customer charges when the project is completed. Electronic switching will greatly increase our[6] capacity to serve our present and future customers.

To avoid any misunderstanding, we are[7] publishing a booklet, *Electronic Switching: What It Means to You.* It will be mailed free of charge to each of our[8] customers. If you have any questions on these important changes after you have read the booklet, please let us know.[9] Yours truly, [182]

5 Dear Mr. Stern: Enclosed is an application form for telephone service for the apartment you plan to rent[1] to college students. The application should be completed and returned as soon as possible.

We are sorry[2] for the delay in installing the telephone in the apartment. Unfortunately, one of our employees[3] was misinformed about the necessity for a deposit. Even though you have been a regular customer[4] of ours for many years, we still require a $50 deposit on an apartment telephone. The[5] deposit will be refunded, of course, when you terminate service. It will not be necessary to furnish[6] our office with the names of the students occupying the apartment.

We appreciate the opportunity[7] of providing telephone service to you and the students in our college community. We will do our[8] best to avoid any possible misunderstandings in the future. Sincerely yours, [176]

6 Miss Poland: As you know, Mrs. Helen Gray will be retiring from the telephone company in November[1] after many years of faithful service. Mrs. Gray's career has been characterized by her constant dedication[2] and professional attitude over the years. She has been an outstanding example for all of us.

Will[3] you please plan a special award for her that could be presented at our annual company banquet in[4] October. We currently have almost $300 in our retirement fund, which should be sufficient for a[5] very special gift for Mrs. Gray.

Please work up a proposal and let me go over it with you sometime next[6] week. Joe Harper [123]

7 Mr. Chan: Last week Harry Edwards and I visited ten telephone companies in three eastern states. At the[1] conclusion of this trip, we determined that our own operations are in sound condition.

There are, however,[2] a few recommendations that we have prepared for the staff. It was our misconception that repair crews should consist[3] of three people, but apparently two are enough. In addition, we should immediately begin the[4] installation of electronic switching equipment in the south end of Baker County. The rapid growth there[5] will soon tax our existing equipment.

In all other areas, it appears that we are efficiently[6] utilizing all our resources. Do you concur with our two general recommendations? Frank Jennings [138]

8 Dear Mr. Sanders: In checking our records, we noticed that your telephone bill is now more than two months overdue.[1] Your current unpaid balance is $82.40, and we have only $25 in[2] your deposit account. This means that we are actually paying for your telephone service.

We must insist that[3] you pay your outstanding balance immediately. Do not make the mistake of delaying. Send us your check. If[4] we do not receive it before September 30, we will be forced to terminate your telephone service. Yours[5] truly,[101]

CHAPTER 7

LESSON 31

3 Dear Mr. Grant: If you are the type of individual who would rather play golf or tennis during your leisure[1] time than spend those long, hot hours keeping your yard in top condition, we have a suggestion for you. Turn over[2] the care and maintenance of your yard at your residence to Green Acres Landscaping Service.

Our staff at Green Acres[3] will install an automatic sprinkling system to keep your lawn looking beautiful. We will spray your yard[4] periodically to kill weeds and insects. In addition, we will mow your lawn weekly and weed your garden areas[5] twice a month. Your yard will be the talk of all the residents in your neighborhood.

What does all this service cost?[6] The cost is probably much less than you think. Visit us at 402 East State Street and let us explain in detail[7] how we can help you eliminate the drudgery of keeping your residence looking beautiful all through[8] the summer. Cordially yours, [165]

4 Dear Miss Chambers: We noticed your advertisement in the *Daily Reporter* for general yard service. We would[1] like you to give us a bid on the landscaping work at our residence at 347 West 23[2] Street.

We would like your estimate to include costs for the following services:

1. Mowing and watering the[3] lawn.
2. Trimming the shrubs.
3. Planting and weeding the garden area.

Please contact us before Friday, February[4] 15; we need to make final arrangements for this work as soon as possible. Cordially yours, [98]

5 Dear Ms. Boyle: Enclosed is the copy of *Total Lawn and Garden Care* that you ordered last month. In your letter you[1] mentioned some specific questions for which you were seeking answers. We want to call your attention to Chapter 5[2] entitled "Insects That Destroy Your Lawn." This chapter identifies the insects that attack your lawn during the[3] growing season and prescribes the treatment necessary to control them.

Please examine the book carefully, and[4] try a few of the ideas it contains. If you are satisfied with it, send us your check for $9.50[5] before April 15. If you are not completely satisfied, just return the book; you will be under no[6] obligation.

We are confident that you will join more than 10,000 other residents in this area[7] who use *Total Lawn and Garden Care* on a daily basis. Sincerely yours, [154]

6 Dear Homeowner: The staff here at Shadow Mountain Nursery would like the residents of the area to have[1] attractively landscaped yards and save money on their heating and air-conditioning bills at the same time. How can[2] we help them accomplish these seemingly unrelated objectives? The answer is quite simple.

A recent study[3] revealed that strategically located shrubs can significantly reduce fuel consumption during the winter[4] months and can keep a residence cooler during the summer. You see, shrubs act as a natural insulating[5] barrier around your residence, and much of the cost of planting them can be recovered through fuel savings.[6]

Call us at 555-9625 and let us explain in detail how we can help you. Sincerely yours, [139]

7 Dear Mr. Smith: If you would like to have a good lawn next spring, now is the time to do something about it. The best[1] way to assure yourself of a lawn that you can be proud of is to let us take care of it.

At a price that is[2] surprisingly low, we will apply the necessary chemicals to your lawn, reseed it, and roll it. Furthermore[3], we will guarantee that in the spring you will have a lawn that will be the talk of all the residents of your[4] neighborhood.

If you will return the enclosed self-addressed card, we will have one of our well-trained, experienced people[5] call at your residence and give you an estimate of the cost. Yours truly, [114]

LESSON 32

3 Dear Ms. Bryan: The cold, harsh winter is the best time of the year to assess the effectiveness of your home's[1] energy-saving properties. Please take a few moments to respond to the following questions:

1. Do you feel cold[2] drafts in your home?
2. Does moisture condense on your windows and sometimes freeze at night?
3. Does your furnace turn on and[3] off repeatedly during cold winter days and nights?
4. Do you feel cooler when standing by your windows than in[4] other parts of your rooms?

If your answers to these questions are yes, perhaps you need to replace the weather stripping[5] around your doors and windows. Weather stripping is easy to install; you can do it yourself. The cost is[6] economical, and the benefits are great.

The next time you are in the Valley View Shopping Mall, drop in to Allen[7] Brothers and let us show you our complete line of energy-saving products for your home. Sincerely yours, [158]

4 Ms. Tate: I recently made a random check of 100 building permits that the city issued last year for[1] the construction of single-family homes. I wanted to determine how many plans called for the use of[2] ceramic tile roofing material. My research disclosed that almost 23 percent did.

The nearest[3] manufacturer of this material is in Troy, which is more than 500 miles away. The tile must be transported[4] by trucks or other vehicles to construction sites here in Springfield.

I believe it would be profitable[5] for us to construct a tile manufacturing plant here in Springfield. If we captured only 50 percent of[6] the existing market, my figures indicate that such a business venture would be successful.

What do you think[7] of this idea? Tom Watson [145]

5 Dear Mr. Miller: In an article in a recent issue of a national periodical, *Future*[1] *America*, Dr. Roy Baird made an interesting observation on the changing designs of today's homes. He[2] said, "In the next decade the exterior of virtually every new home will be constructed of maintenance-free[3] materials."

The only quarrel we have with that statement is the time frame the author suggests. Today many[4] new homes are built with a wide array of maintenance-free materials on all exterior surfaces.[5] This satisfies a critical demand homeowners have expressed for many years.

When you decide to build your dream[6] home, stop in at United Builders and let us show you some of the new products that will enable you to build[7] a beautiful, trouble-free home. Sincerely yours, [149]

6 Dear Mr. Edwards: If you do not

have double glass windows in your home, perhaps you have noticed that it is often[1] drafty and uncomfortable. In addition, your fuel bills may be unusually high. With escalating[2] costs, it makes no sense to use fuel needlessly.

Did you know that the cost of installing windows from Birmingham Glass[3] Company can be recovered in a few years' time through the savings on your fuel bills? Our double glass windows come[4] in various thicknesses. They come with wood or aluminum frames. They are made to the exact specifications[5] of your home and can be installed in just a few hours.

Call us at 555-3845 for a free[6] estimate of the cost of making your home a more comfortable and less costly place in which to live. Yours truly,[7] [140]

7 Dear Mr. Martin: Ask yourself these questions that relate to the security of your home:

1. Is my house often[1] empty during the prime weekday burglary hours of 9 a.m. to 5 p.m.?
2. Am I near a major[2] highway?
3. Is the front or back of my house secluded?

If your answer to any of these critical questions[3] is yes, your house needs the protection provided by a Madison Security System. This system can stop[4] even the most skillful thieves and vandals.

For a free estimate of the cost of installing a Madison[5] Security System, call us at 555-9206. A well-trained, experienced engineer will visit[6] you at your convenience and give you complete information. Yours very truly, [134]

LESSON 33

3 Dear Mrs. Chang: Most people, of course, would like to have fine, elegant furniture in their homes. If you have checked prices[1] recently, however, you know that a houseful of high-quality furniture can cost $10,000[2] or more.

The Denver Community College is offering a short course in furniture building and repair. The[3] course will be taught at the main building at 340 State Street. The teacher will be Mr. James Smith, one of the best-known[4] furniture experts in the area.

Building furniture yourself is a relaxing, enjoyable hobby,[5] and it can save you money. Many of our former students have actually built most of the furniture in[6] their homes at less than 50 percent of the cost of purchasing it at a retail store.

Because we want to give[7] individual attention to each person, this class will be limited to 20 students. We feel that there[8] will be many more students who want to take the class than we can accommodate. Therefore, if you are interested[9] in the course, call us today; we will send you the necessary registration forms immediately. Sincerely[10] yours, [201]

4 Dear Mr. Fox: We received notice in the mail today that the two chandeliers you ordered for the living room[1] of your new home are not presently available. These fixtures are manufactured in Rome, Italy, and a[2] labor strike there has temporarily halted production.

We regret this delay, and we fear that it will be[3] the end of the summer before these fixtures will be available. Please let us know if you would like us to pursue[4] our efforts to purchase these particular chandeliers or if you would prefer to come to our showroom and[5] make another selection. Sincerely yours, [108]

5 Dear Miss Evans: Nothing can improve the looks of the interior of your home or make it a more comfortable[1] place in which to live than good carpeting. We feel you will find the best selection of high-quality carpeting[2] at the lowest prices in town at Adams Carpet Company.

We recently surveyed five other carpet[3] stores here in Houston, Texas, to compare our prices with theirs on identical products. We discovered that eight[4] of our carpets were sold by the competing companies. Our average prices were 23 percent lower than[5] those of the other stores. In fact, the prices of our closest competitor were 13 percent higher than ours.[6]

When you couple our low prices with the fine services we provide, we feel you will be convinced that Adams Carpet[7] Company is the place to go for all your carpeting needs. Sincerely yours, [154]

6 Dear Dr. Martinez: In order to serve the future needs of our customers in southern Louisiana,[1] we have opened a sales office in New Orleans. Mr. Jason Casey is the manager of this office. Mr.[2] Casey has been in the furniture business for many years. Before joining our organization, he worked[3] in the auditing, accounting, and sales divisions of the National Furniture Company. I am sure he[4] can be of great assistance to you whenever you are in the market for new furniture.

Please do not hesitate[5] to call on Mr. Casey for any information about our line of quality furniture. Sincerely[6] yours, [121]

LESSON 34

Office-Style Dictation

1 *(As dictated)* Dear Mrs. Moore: Thank you for your order of Monday, July 12. (No, that should be *13*.) We were, of course, very glad to receive it.

Unfortunately, we are out of some of the items you want now, (Make that *at the present time*.) but we should have them in a few days. You can be sure that we will send you all of the items (Change that to *things*; oh, leave it *items*.) you want just as soon as we receive them in stock.

I am enclosing a copy of our new catalog. (Make that *latest catalog*.) I am sure you will enjoy looking through it. Thanks for your understanding. Sincerely yours,

(1) *(As it would be transcribed)* Dear Mrs. Moore: Thank you for your order of Monday, July 13. We were, of course, very glad to receive it.[1]

Unfortunately, we are out of some of the items you want at the present time, but we should have them in a[2] few days. You can be sure that we will send you all of the items you want just as soon as we receive them in stock.[3]

I am enclosing a copy of our latest catalog. I am sure you will enjoy looking through it. Thanks for[4] your understanding. Sincerely yours, [87]

3 Dear Mr. Lester: This year's Parade of Homes will be held in the Valley View subdivision just south of Central[1] Community College. The opening is scheduled for 9 a.m. on May 15, and we certainly hope that[2] you will be able to spend some time with us.

The entries this year are among the most outstanding we have ever[3] had. Fourteen of the best, most experienced contractors in the area have built homes that you are sure to find[4] interesting and unusual.

The theme of this year's Parade of Homes is "Planning for Tomorrow." Several of[5] the houses incorporate solar heating and cooling systems. We think you will be impressed by their sensible[6] design, beauty, and style.

The judging of the homes will take place on Monday, May 14; all awards will be posted[7] for the entire week. Make your plans to be with us sometime during the week; we will be looking forward to seeing[8] you. Sincerely yours, [164]

4 Dear Mrs. Turner: I am planning to construct a home in Green Acres during the coming year. I plan to do[1] some of the construction work myself, but I need some vital information before I proceed.

I am presently[2] shopping for heating and air-conditioning systems. I have read a number of articles in recent[3] magazines about the benefits of various types of systems. Frankly, however, I am puzzled as to the[4] best, most economical system for my particular needs.

Enclosed is a preliminary sketch of the[5] plans for my home. The house will face east on Elm Drive. Will you please provide me with information on the major[6] advantages and disadvantages of the following heating and cooling systems: gas, electric, hot water,[7] and solar.

From my experience with your firm, I am confident that I can rely on the information[8] you will provide. I appreciate your assistance in this matter, Mrs. Turner. Sincerely yours, [178]

5 Dear Frank: In the June issue of *Great American Homes* several pages were devoted to a unique home[1] designed and built by William Brown of Vail, Colorado. Mr. Brown built his home with double walls that had six inches[2] of air space between them for insulation. The ceilings and floors were very well insulated also. On[3] the south side of the two-story home, he constructed a beautifully designed greenhouse that contained a solar heating[4] system. Last winter Mr. Brown's heating bill was substantially below the average for his part of the country.[5]

I am excited about Mr. Brown's ideas, and I believe they would work here in our locality[6] equally well. I have sent for further information on this and other homes designed by Mr. Brown.

I would like[7] to talk with you as soon as possible about incorporating some of the concepts in the house I plan to[8] construct in the near future. Will you please let me know when it will be convenient for you to meet with me to discuss[9] these plans. Sincerely yours, [185]

6 Dear Dr. Carter: Are your jewels, insurance policies, and other valuable items safe in your home? They are[1] if they are kept in a Boyd safe, which sets off an alarm when it is opened, moved, or lifted.

The Boyd safe has a[2] combination lock and a key lock as well; only you can open it. It is roomy too; it has more than enough[3] space to hold all the things that are worth protecting.

Get a Boyd safe today. It is for sale at all the stores listed[4] on the enclosed circular. Sincerely yours, [89]

7 Dear Mr. Gomez: Government figures prove that you can save as much as 15 percent on your heating bills by[1] cleaning your chimney and furnace every year. A clean heating system will not only save you a significant[2] amount on your heating bills but will also help to prevent fires and explosions.

It doesn't make sense to take any[3] risks when it costs only $57 to be safe. That is what we charge to do the following things:[4]

1. Clean your furnace with special brushes.

2. Clean the pipes leading from the furnace to the chimney.

3. Clean the entire[5] chimney.

Mail the enclosed card today telling us when it will be convenient for you to have us do this work[6] for you. Sincerely yours, [124]

LESSON 35

3 Dear Mr. Hastings: Do you dislike the looks of your yard? Do you dislike the appearance of your garden area?[1] If you do, our company can help you do something about the problem. Our organization, Modern Yard[2] Enterprises, has a complete line of yard furniture and recreational equipment for both children and adults.[3] Our products provide a natural complement to the beauty of your property.

We have a complete line[4] of the latest, most up-to-date yard furniture. In addition, we can construct patios, swimming pools, and tennis[5] courts. Our expert personnel can install most of our products without displacing any of your shrubs or trees.[6]

We would welcome the opportunity of analyzing your needs with you and your family, Mr. Hastings.[7] If you will return the enclosed self-addressed card, one of our representatives will contact you in the near future.[8] Cordially yours, [164]

4 Dear Mr. Norris: One of the fastest-growing sports in the United States today is tennis. Municipalities[1] are having a difficult time keeping pace with the demand for new, modern tennis courts.

As a result,[2] private clubs are being organized in many areas. Although these clubs are successful, profitable[3] financial ventures, their membership fees are usually very high. Many prospective members are quite disillusioned[4] when they realize just how much membership actually costs.

Have you ever considered the alternative of[5] owning your own private tennis court? If you have the room, this could be the best possible investment you could make[6] in family entertainment. In addition, you could add substantially to the value of your property.[7]

Would you be willing to spend half an hour with Mr. Gary Nelson, our sales manager, to learn how our company[8] can quickly and easily build a top-quality tennis court right in the privacy of your own backyard?[9] Write us or call 555-4569 for further details. Sincerely yours, [194]

5 Dear Mr. Tracy: Stereos Unlimited is currently holding the biggest sale in our history. When[1] you come to our store, you can disregard all regular price tags; everything is reduced up to 50 percent.[2] Wouldn't a high-quality built-in stereo system for your home or office add an important dimension[3] to the hours you spend there?

Our best stereo system is comprised of a radio, a cassette tape player, and[4] four large speakers, which can be placed in any location you choose.

If you buy one of our stereo systems before[5] Friday, September 12, we will give you a tape player for your automobile and your choice of any three[6] tapes in our store. Yours truly, [125]

6 Dear Mrs. Masters: A few weeks ago my roof developed a leak that has caused some damage to the walls, ceiling,[1] and carpeting in my living room. I have contacted the roofing contractor, who gave me a bid of[2] $1,000 to repair the damage.

According to the provisions of my insurance policy with your[3] organization, the National Insurance Company, this kind of loss is covered. I called your office three times,[4] and each time I was told that someone would take care of my claim. However, no one has done so. I realize you are[5] busy, but I am discouraged.

Will you please send one of your claims adjusters to my home immediately. I[6] am eager to have the repair work done. Sincerely yours, [130]

7 Dear Mrs. Day: Is your basement always damp, musty, and disagreeable? Does water seeping into your basement[1] prevent you from turning it into a comfortable, enjoyable playroom in which your family could[2] enjoy many happy hours?

If this is so, return the enclosed card immediately requesting a copy of our[3] booklet, *Davis Waterproofing Guide.* It will tell you how you can stop leaks once and for all by utilizing Davis[4] products. The booklet was prepared by experts in the field, and their directions are easy to follow.

Take the[5] initial step in making your basement a place that your family will enjoy; return the enclosed card today,[6] Mrs. Day. Cordially yours, [125]

8 Dear Ms. Yale: Please consider this letter my resignation as manager of the Yale Hardware Company. I[1] would like the resignation to take effect on Friday, June 10, if it is convenient for you.

Two of my friends[2] and I have organized a new company known as the Home Remodeling Company. Our offices are[3] located at 416 West 42 Street in Fairfield. We will specialize in remodeling and[4] redecorating homes. We will buy many of our supplies from your company, and I hope you will recommend our[5] organization to your customers. We guarantee you that they will not be disappointed with our work.

I enjoyed[6] my years in the employ of the Yale Hardware Company, and I wish your company success in the future.[7] Sincerely yours, [143]

9 Dear Mr. Johnson: Wouldn't you like the thrill of being able to tell a friend who admired a cabinet in[1] your living room, I made that myself"? Perhaps you have always wished that you could make things but felt that you didn't have[2] the talent and ability.

If you will give yourself an opportunity, you may find that you can make almost[3] any piece of furniture that you desire to make. How can you give yourself this chance? Invest in a copy[4] of *The Furniture Manual.* This book will show you step by step how to make more than 50 different pieces of[5] furniture.

Send for a copy today; you will not be disappointed with it. Sincerely yours, [117]

CHAPTER 8

LESSON 36

3 Dear Mr. Benton: Thank you for your letter of inquiry about Ms. Mary Cunningham, one of my former[1] faculty members here at the Eastern School of Culinary Arts. I am very happy to give her an unqualified[2] recommendation.

Ms. Cunningham joined our staff on September 1, 1977, and taught[3] here until last year. We found her to be quite adept at adjusting to various situations. In addition,[4] she was quite popular with the faculty, the staff, and the students. Ms. Cunningham made a number of[5] recommendations concerning the operation of our school, and I am happy to say we adopted most[6] of them.

I am sure that if you hire Ms. Cunningham, you will be quite happy with her work. Sincerely yours, [138]

4 Dear Mr. Gomez: Thank you very much for sending me your comments about the cooking course that the National[1] Department Store sponsors each year. We are very happy that you enjoyed the course this year, and we believe that the[2] recommendations you made for improving the course are very good.

Unfortunately, we cannot adopt

all of[3] the recommendations because we have a limited staff and a strict budget. However, we plan to adapt[4] one or two of your suggestions to fit our particular needs and our budget.

If you have any further[5] suggestions you would like to make, I hope you will feel free to send them to me. I will be very glad to receive them.[6] Yours truly, [122]

5 Dear Mr. Taylor: As you know, many items sold in grocery stores have magnetic codes imprinted on the[1] containers. These markings can contribute to the efficiency of any store. Just how can they do this?

The checkout[2] personnel can use special light pens to read the codes. Each item is added to the customer's cash register[3] tape. A brief description of the item and the price appear in easy-to-read type. When all items have been[4] registered, the bill is totaled quickly and accurately. All this can be accomplished in a fraction of the[5] time it takes even the most adept person to perform the functions manually.

If your grocery store is[6] not now taking advantage of the special markings that are already on most of the containers, now is the[7] time to take action. Write to us today; one of our well-trained, experienced representatives will be glad to[8] come to your store to speak with you personally. Very sincerely yours, [173]

6 Dear Mr. Pulaski: Thank you for your letter asking my opinion of the General computer system[1] that we are using to help speed up the operations of our food store.

As you know, we installed the computer[2] six months ago. We were not able to adopt the standard program, but we were able to adapt it[3] successfully to fit our own needs. At first we had a number of problems. However, most of the trouble has been[4] corrected, and we are very happy with the computer and with our new procedures.

The major advantages[5] of using the computer are as follows:

1. We are able to keep our inventory under much better[6] control.

2. We have been able to save at least five minutes' time for each person at the checkout register.[7]

3. We have fewer complaints about overcharging.

Unfortunately, we have not been able to decrease our[8] overall expenses, but we feel that we will be able to lower our costs significantly within the[9] next year or so.

If you would like to visit our store and see the computer in operation, we will be happy[10] to have you as our guest. Sincerely yours, [208]

7 Dear Mr. Harding: We are delighted to announce the opening of our new self-service food store in your[1] neighborhood. The store is located at 402 Third Avenue, which is only a few blocks from your home.

As you[2] probably know, we have operated food stores throughout the Atlanta, Georgia, area for many years.[3] However, this is the first to be opened in your neighborhood. Many years ago we adopted the policy[4] of selling only the finest foods at the very lowest prices possible. We are happy to be able[5] to continue this tradition in the new store.

During the first week we will be offering special buys on fruits,[6] vegetables, and meats. In addition, you will be able to make substantial savings on many nonfood items.[7] Come in anytime during the week of August 6 and see for yourself what wonderful savings you can make.[8] Very sincerely yours, [164]

LESSON 37

3 Dear Mr. Howard: One of the most difficult tasks we face at Superior Food Markets is finding adequately[1] trained personnel. Presently our demand for checkers greatly exceeds the supply, and the prospect of hiring[2] experienced people to fill these positions is bleak.

Because you are director of the state employment[3] service, we hope you will be willing to set up a training program for those who would like to learn how to check[4] groceries.

If your office could administer qualifying tests and provide a short training course, we could be reasonably[5] sure that those people you refer to us will succeed in their work. We would, of course, be happy to pay all costs[6] involved.

We now need at least 50 well-trained people for positions in our grocery chain. If you are willing[7] to work with us in this venture, please let us know as soon as possible. Cordially yours, [156]

4 Dear Miss Sutton: We are pleased to tell you that you have been accepted in our home economics graduate program[1] for the coming school year. A teaching grant for $5,000 has been approved by the dean of admissions.[2] We will proceed to work out your assignments and will contact you as soon as our schedule is finalized.

As you[3] know, our program is designed not only for secondary school teachers but also for consultants, salespeople,[4] and researchers.

The enclosed brochure contains a list of both on- and off-campus living accommodations and[5] a calendar of special events for the coming year.

We are looking forward to getting acquainted with you[6] at our first general staff meeting on Tuesday, September 15, at 8 a.m. in the main auditorium[7] at 402 East Elm Drive. Sincerely yours, [149]

5 Dear Miss Green: The sales of Powers Frozen Dinners have fallen 16 percent during the past year. We had predicted[1] that our sales of these dinners would exceed our record-setting sales of two years ago, but we were quite wrong.

In[2] an attempt to find the reason for this alarming trend, we hired a marketing research firm to study the problem.[3] They concluded that a great deal of customer resistance is caused by the package we use for our dinners.[4] They contend that the package lacks appeal, and that contention is substantiated by their opinion survey.[5]

Would your company be interested in designing a new package for our frozen dinners? We are now revising[6] our entire advertising program, and we hope the new package will play a major role in the effectiveness[7] of that program. Will you please let us hear from you as soon as possible. Sincerely yours, [157]

6 Dear Mr. Temple: These days the newspapers are full of advertisements for quick, easy ways to lose weight. Special[1] low-calorie snacks and a variety of unusual diets are among the numerous schemes for which[2] Americans pay millions of dollars each year.

The truth of the matter is that body weight can ordinarily[3] reflect only two factors. These factors are the food we eat and the calories we burn. At the Washington[4] Institute we help you develop a balance between these two important elements. We will plan an exercise[5] routine that will help you feel and look better. More important, however, we will tailor a diet especially[6] for you to help you succeed in achieving your most desirable weight.

There is no cost or obligation[7] for your initial visit; we hope to see you soon. Sincerely yours, [153]

7 Dear Mr. Knight: Would you be interested in displaying your health food products during the Virginia Education[1] Association convention in October?

Thousands of teachers attend this two-day meeting each year. They[2] come seeking new ideas and looking for new products to help them do their jobs more effectively. Most manufacturers[3] of educational products concede that state conventions provide more exposure for their goods and[4] services than any other single medium could do.

I have enclosed a brief questionnaire and an updated[5] fee schedule that supersedes any prior schedules you may possess. Please complete the questionnaire and return it[6] before April 15 if you plan to display your products during our October convention. Sincerely yours,[7] [140]

LESSON 38

3 Dear Mr. Carter: When I hear a newscast, I want today's news; I do not want last week's. When I buy a calculator,[1] I want it to be an up-to-date model that will perform the operations I require. When I buy[2] an expensive suit or sports coat, I expect it to be stylish and durable. It seems reasonable, therefore,[3] that when I purchase dairy products at your supermarket, Mr. Carter, I expect them to be fresh and wholesome.[4]

Three times during the past month I checked the dates on the milk in your dairy case and found they had already expired.[5] Each time it was necessary for me to go to another store to make my milk purchases.

If you are[6] not able to maintain fresh milk in your store, it may be necessary for me to do all my shopping elsewhere.[7] I hope that this action will not become necessary. Cordially yours, [153]

4 Dear Ms. Swift: The enclosed brochure will acquaint you with our new home economics publication,

New Ways To Prepare[1] *Food.* This book was written by Alice Golden, one of the country's foremost food experts, and was designed especially[2] as a resource for college cooking classes. However, it may be used in any way that you wish.

This[3] text contains 500 pages and more than 100,000 words. It has almost 800 beautiful[4] illustrations. To help you review the book, Miss Golden has prepared an examination guide consisting of[5] 100 questions relating directly to the material in the text.

Please examine the brochure carefully.[6] If you would like to examine a copy of *New Ways To Prepare Food,* just return the attached coupon. We[7] will send you an examination copy immediately. If you like the book, keep it; we will bill you later.[8] If you are displeased with the book in any way, just return it to us when you have completed your[9] examination. You will be under no obligation, of course. Sincerely yours, [194]

5 Dear Mr. Poland: Approximately 20 percent of the people in our city are eligible to[1] participate in our programs for senior citizens. Our recent studies indicate, however, that only[2] about half of these people are taking advantage of the programs.

Last week we called several people who had[3] not visited our center for more than a month to determine the reasons for their absence. Almost every one[4] of them reported that lack of transportation was the major cause.

If there is any way we can find the funds,[5] we should purchase a bus for the exclusive use of the senior citizens of our community. Will you please[6] consider this suggestion and give me your recommendation sometime before the end of the month. Sincerely[7] yours, [141]

6 Dear Mr. Park: Would you like to save at least 50 percent on the everyday cost of the meat, poultry, and fish[1] that your family consumes? Most people would, and it is easier to do than you might believe.

Simply drive up[2] the Hamilton Freeway to the River Ranch exit any day from 8 a.m. to 3 p.m. and purchase the[3] beef, poultry, or fish of your choice at the Country Market. We sell our products at about half the prices charged by[4] the city supermarkets. You can take your purchases home with you, or you can have them delivered for a small[5] fee.

Hundreds of people save money by shopping at the Country Market every day. Maybe you should too. Anyway,[6] you should visit our store at least once to see for yourself the wonderful bargains that we offer. Yours very[7] truly, [141]

LESSON 39

Office-Style Dictation

1 *(As dictated)* Dear Mr. Madison: This is to acknowledge receipt of your letter asking for a recommendation for Miss Jane Washington, who formerly worked for my company. I am very happy to give Miss Washington a good recommendation.

Miss Washington began working

for me about five years ago. She worked in the accounting department and in the billing department. (Make that *in the billing department and in the accounting department*.) Each of her supervisors found her to be a cooperative and efficient employee. (Make that *an efficient and cooperative employee*.)

Miss Washington came to us from the General Manufacturing Company in Trenton, where she worked for several years after graduating from college. (Put that last sentence before the one beginning *Miss Washington began working....*)

I am sure, Mr. Madison, that you will be making no mistake if you hire Miss Washington. Sincerely yours,

1 *(As it would be transcribed)* Dear Mr. Madison: This is to acknowledge receipt of your letter asking for a recommendation for[1] Miss Jane Washington, who formerly worked for my company. I am very happy to give Miss Washington a[2] good recommendation.

Miss Washington came to us from the General Manufacturing Company in Trenton,[3] where she worked for several years after graduating from college. Miss Washington began working for me[4] about five years ago. She worked in the billing department and in the accounting department. Each of her[5] supervisors found her to be an efficient and cooperative employee.

I am sure, Mr. Madison, that[6] you will be making no mistake if you hire Miss Washington. Sincerely yours, [134]

3 Dear Mr. Robbins: Our present dilemma reminds us of the children's story of the little red hen. She tried[1] to persuade the other barnyard animals to help her plant, tend, and harvest the wheat so that she could make bread.[2] However, no one would willingly help. But when the loaves were ready to eat, the animals did show an interest.

We[3] have over 150 acres of sweet apple trees that must be fertilized, pruned, watered, and picked. We know[4] that almost everyone likes to buy fresh apples from supermarkets and roadside stands, but our crop will not be[5] available this summer unless we get immediate help.

Can you channel the efforts of your staff at the[6] Temporary Employment Service toward helping us hire full-time and part-time workers for our orchards? Without your[7] assistance, we may not be able to provide the delicious fruit our customers have come to expect. Sincerely[8] yours, [161]

4 Dear Mr. Brooks: As a new resident of our farming community, perhaps you have asked yourself, "Why should I[1] join the Farmers' Cooperative?"

First, the Farmers' Cooperative is owned by its members and exists solely to[2] serve their needs. Second, it stocks every type of equipment you will ever use in your operations. Third, it provides[3] processing services and storage facilities for your produce. Fourth, the cooperative guarantees you[4] the highest prices available when you market your farm goods. Finally, because the

Farmers' Cooperative[5] is a non-profit organization, any money we make above expenses is returned to the members.[6]

To become a member, just fill out the enclosed application form and return it to us. Our board of directors[7] will process it at its next monthly meeting. Sincerely yours, [152]

5 Dear Miss Sota: Would you be available to serve as a judge for the Utah Livestock Show on July 15,[1] 16, and 17 in Salt Lake City? You have done an excellent job as a judge in the past, and we hope[2] you will accept our invitation again this year.

Preliminary judging will take place on the 15th and[3] 16th; final competition will be on the 17th. It would be necessary, therefore, for you to be[4] available during at least one day of the preliminary events as well as for the finals.

Please let[5] us know before June 1 if we can count on your help during this outstanding livestock show. Cordially yours, [118]

6 Dear Mr. Tate: The importance of the American farmer in our country's economic affairs has never[1] been quite so apparent as it is today. Because of several years' deficits in our international[2] balance of payments, we must increase exports if we are to reverse the trend. Food is one product that we produce[3] efficiently and abundantly.

American farmers continue to be among the most efficient[4] workers in the world, and this productivity can help us to balance our budgets in the future.

In your[5] position as executive secretary of the National Farming Alliance, you can do much to develop[6] profitable foreign markets through which our wide variety of food commodities can be exported.[7] We appreciated your outstanding efforts in the past, and we want you to know that your government officials[8] stand ready to assist you in your endeavors to promote the sale of food throughout the world. Cordially[9] yours, [181]

7 Dear Mr. Waters: If you have been delaying your decision to become a member of the National Farming[1] Organization, perhaps now is the time to take action and join one of the fastest-growing associations[2] in America.

As a member of the National Farming Organization, you receive the[3] following benefits:

1. Political strength to help farmers realize important local and national objectives.[4]
2. A purchasing program that will save you money on almost every commodity you buy for your farm.[5]
3. A steady supply of up-to-date, valuable information on which you can base the important economic[6] decisions you must make.

Our membership application is enclosed with this letter. Fill it out now and[7] return it to us along with your membership fee of $85. Sincerely yours, [157]

LESSON 40

3 Dear Mr. James: I have decided

to retire and discontinue my canning business. As you may remember,[1] I have operated the cannery since January 1, 1960, in Ocean City. During[2] this time I have expanded the plant three times to keep up with the demands of the fishing industry. Originally,[3] I canned only salmon. During the past few years, however, I have expanded the operation to[4] include canning shrimp, tuna, and several other varieties of fish.

My equipment and machinery[5] are still in excellent condition, and business was better last year than ever before. However, the irregular[6] hours and demanding work schedule have prompted my decision to retire.

Are you still interested in either[7] purchasing or leasing the business? If you are, please contact me before the end of January. I need[8] to make arrangements soon so that the cannery will be in full operation when the fishing season starts in[9] just a few months. Cordially yours, [186]

4 Dear Mr. Adams: Local farmers are receiving a great deal of criticism because of the rapid[1] increases in food prices at the grocery store. Could our local association become actively involved[2] in a publicity campaign to counteract this criticism?

There is no real basis for the criticism;[3] it developed irrespective of the actual facts. Our own farm periodicals indicate that[4] Americans are now spending only about 15 percent of their incomes on food, and that percentage has not[5] changed appreciably during the past ten years. During this time farmers' incomes have risen much slower than have food[6] marketing costs. Consequently, we feel that the current criticism is unwarranted.

Please consider this[7] item at your next meeting and let us know your reaction. Cordially yours, [154]

5 Dear Mr. Clay: If you could design the perfect farm tractor, what features would you build into it? Would you be concerned[1] with comfort and convenience? Would you want to be able to plow or harvest all day without undue fatigue?[2] Would you want gauges on the control panel to be neatly grouped and easily accessible? Would you want to[3] be able to use the tractor for many years without finding that it had broken down and had become[4] irreparable?

If these factors are important to you, we invite you to examine the new line of King tractors.[5] King tractors are years ahead of their time in design and function.

Stop in sometime soon and see for yourself what our[6] designers have done to make farming easier and more profitable. Sincerely yours, [136]

6 Dear Member: The fourth annual Farm Implement Show will be held this year in Great Falls, Montana, on November[1] 6, 7, and 8. The exhibits will open at 12 noon each day and will close at 10 p.m.

Thirteen major[2] manufacturers are participating in this year's show. They will feature the latest developments in all[3] types of farm machinery. The sales representatives for the companies will be on hand to provide you with[4] all the information you need.

We hope you will take a day or two to visit the exhibits during this[5] outstanding show. Sincerely yours,
[105]

7 Dear Ms. Slater: The state of Washington provides a wide variety of services to fruit and vegetable[1] growers. We would be happy to add your name to our mailing list, as you requested, to receive the publications[2] we distribute on the care of fruit trees. We will inform you of the proper planting times, the types of[3] insecticides to use, and the correct time to pick the fruit.

When fruit trees are not properly cared for, the insects they[4] harbor can spread to neighboring trees and cause irreparable damage. It is imperative, therefore, that all fruit[5] growers do their part in stopping the spread of harmful disease.

We commend you for your interest and will provide[6] whatever assistance we can to keep your trees healthy and productive. Sincerely yours,
[135]

CHAPTERS 9-16
Lessons 41-80
PART

CHAPTER 9

LESSON 41

3 Dear Mr. Franklin: I have both a checking and a savings account at your branch of the American National[1] Bank in Reading, Pennsylvania. I am making plans for a vacation in Europe this summer, and I[2] recently purchased some traveler's checks from your bank.

It occurred to me that I do not know what to do if I need[3] additional money during my stay in Europe. Are there banks in Europe that will cash personal checks written[4] on an account with the American National Bank in Reading? Do you think that it would be helpful to take[5] a letter of credit from you?

Thank you for a prompt reply, Mr. Franklin. Sincerely yours, [117]

4 Dear Mr. Gray: You have probably read in the local newspaper that all branches of the Second National[1] Bank of Seattle, Washington, are now permitted by the government to pay a higher interest rate on time[2] certificates of $5,000.

Because you and your wife frequently invest in time certificates, we[3] thought you would want to be reminded of the possibility of added earnings. If you have any surplus[4] money to invest, now would be the time to invest it. You will, of course, receive a higher rate of interest on[5] a five-year certificate than you will on a one-year certificate.

If we can be of further assistance[6] to you in investing your funds, please call us at 555-6491. If you make your deposit by[7] September 1, we will show our appreciation by giving you a small silver serving plate. Sincerely yours, [159]

5 Gentlemen: Several professors at the college in Portland have expressed an interest in starting a combination[1] savings and retirement plan with the Oregon Funding Association. Professor Dennis O'Brien,[2] head of the English department, has been elected president of this group.

These professors are interested[3] in a plan whereby they can each deposit from $100 to $200 a month and have you[4] invest it in stocks or mutual funds for them. They are also interested in having their deposits[5] automatically withheld from their paychecks and deposited directly to their accounts with your association.[6]

If you have such savings plans, may they be used as retirement programs? What is the rate of interest the association[7] pays? When may a professor start retirement payments?

The group of professors would like to have this program[8] go into effect by the first of the year. Since this is the month of October, they would appreciate receiving[9] answers to the above questions within the next week or so. They would also appreciate receiving any[10] other information or advice you may be able to give them. In addition, please send me copies of[11] any information you send to Professor O'Brien.

Professor O'Brien and his committee are[12] anxiously awaiting your reply. Yours very truly, [250]

6 Dear Student: The First National City Bank of Albany is glad to welcome you to State College and to our[1] fine city. You are no doubt concerned about what banking services are available to you and which bank you[2] should select.

We hope you will consider doing business with the First National City Bank of Albany. We[3] have many advantages for the students at State College:

1. We are located close to the main campus.
2.[4] We offer fast, friendly service.
3. We accept applications from students for short- and long-term loans.
4. We print[5] your checks for a nominal fee and include your name, your student identification number, and your address[6] at no extra cost.

We hope you will stop in at First National and let us help you with your banking needs. Cordially[7] yours, [141]

7 Ladies and Gentlemen: If you are planning to expand your business or replace furnishings or equipment, our[1] loan manager, Mr. Paul Johnson, will be delighted to explain our services to you in detail.

Mr.[2] Johnson had been a loan officer with the Nevada Savings and Loan Association for eight years before[3] being promoted to his current position as loan manager. Therefore, he has had a great deal of experience[4] helping organizations determine how much added capital they will need in order to make their[5] projected changes. Mr. Johnson is also skilled at arranging long-term loans for companies. He is adept[6] at handling special situations that might arise.

If you are contemplating changes within your company,[7] do not hesitate to let our loan manager explain our convenient terms. Cordially yours, [157]

LESSON 42

3 Ladies and Gentlemen: Enclosed is the completed application blank that you asked me to submit for your[1] consideration. You will notice that I have an impeccable, unmarred credit record. Smith and Company has[2] actively progressed under my ownership and direction for the past ten years. During that time the company[3] has made tremendous gains in inventory and sales. Twice we expanded the building that we now occupy; we[4] are a growing, successful, and progressive organization.

When we talked yesterday about my obtaining[5] a loan from the Management Funding Corporation, I mentioned that we need a low-interest loan in order to[6] expand for the third time. I would be happy to supply any further financial information that you may[7] need.

Thank you for acting quickly on this loan application. Sincerely yours, [154]

4 Dear Mr. Scott: You have been my financial advisor for many years and have always given me sound advice.[1] I am now planning to remodel my residence, and I need your assistance. Do you know where I can obtain[2] a home-improvement loan? I prefer to work with a lending institution that expedites the issuance of[3] loans and eliminates red tape. You are aware, of course, that I am a very good credit risk.

I am interested[4] in adding a family room to my house, and I want to begin construction by Monday, November 2.[5] I am interested in obtaining a low-cost loan because this fall I will have the additional expense of[6] sending my oldest son to college.

Any information you can supply will be greatly appreciated,[7] Mr. Scott. Cordially yours, [145]

5 Ladies and Gentlemen: No doubt you have seen the advertisements in the *Journal* indicating that we are a[1] new lending institution in the Tacoma, Washington, area. We are inviting a select few[2] corporate directors to come to our bank on Thursday, June 15, to learn more about the services we offer[3] businesses. We want to take this opportunity to extend a special invitation for you to be with[4] us. We will explain completely our low-cost programs for financing inventory, remodeling office[5] facilities, and purchasing new, modern equipment. At the meeting we will invite your inquiry on all types[6] of secured business loans.

You will find our interest rates low and our terms flexible. In addition, should you wish to[7] borrow money at our bank, you will not be required to supply a financial statement before your application[8] is considered.

If your organization is planning to increase its inventory, remodel your[9] facilities, or purchase new equipment, we hope you will attend our interesting, informative session on Thursday[10] at 9 a.m. Yours truly, [208]

6 Dear Dr. Jackson: We are happy to have you as a new depositor in our local bank. Mrs. Wallace,[1] our customer relations officer, will be available to help you with your needs at any time.

As you[2] may know, we have over 30,000 satisfied depositors at the Phoenix branch of the Arizona[3] State Bank. This number is constantly growing, and we are sure that the increase in the number of depositors[4] is caused by the many services we offer our customers.

The attached brochure explains that all our banking[5] business is regulated by the Federal Deposit Insurance Corporation. The FDIC insures[6] to $100,000 the amount of money in your savings account. We are a full-service bank, and[7] we offer you many special services.

If you have any questions, Dr. Jackson, about your investments[8] at the Phoenix branch, please call Mrs. Wallace. She and the other officers of our bank are always happy to[9] be of service to you. Sincerely yours, [187]

7 Dear Mr. and Mrs. Grant: Welcome to the Green Acres Development. We know you will enjoy your new home and[1] its nicely planned surroundings.

Before you start the landscaping of your new yard, let us invite you to come to the[2] Jackson Landscaping and Irrigation Company at 324 South Pine Street and let us explain to you[3] the many varieties of sprinkler systems that we install and maintain.

We have had ten years' experience[4] in landscaping yards and installing sprinkler systems. Let us help you solve the problem of starting a new yard.[5]

Incidentally, we offer many payment plans tailored to fit any budget. We hope you will come in soon.[6] Sincerely yours, [122]

LESSON 43

3 Ladies and Gentlemen: Recently I misplaced my copy of the regular annual financial report[1] of the Cunningham Company. Will you please send me another copy as soon as possible.

I have been pleased[2] with the quarterly return from my 145 shares of common stock. The stock split last quarter was a[3] welcome one; I think it characterizes the good health of the company.

Thank you for your help. Sincerely yours,[4] [80]

4 Gentlemen: In 1972 your bank issued an annuity contract to me; I have been making[1] regular payments on my contract No. 12145.

Because I am now making plans to retire within[2] the next year, I would like one of your officers to gather all the data relating to this contract so[3] that I can discuss the various payment options that are open to me. My main interest, of course, is to choose[4] the plan that will give me the greatest tax advantage.

I will be in San Francisco, California, on Monday[5] morning, February 7, to discuss the matter. I hope that one of your staff members will be able to[6] get the information together in order to discuss my annuity contract and my retirement plans[7] with me. Very truly yours, [145]

5 To the Board: As you will remember, on Thursday, December 13, our board of directors voted to sell our[1] stock in the City Insurance Company. For the past three years, the City Insurance Company stock has decreased[2] in value, and we felt that it would not be wise to continue to hold this stock.

The price on Thursday was[3] $50 per share, and we held 1,000 shares. Unfortunately, we did not ask our financial advisors[4] to sell the stock until Monday, December 17; the delay was a costly one for us. Over the weekend[5] the stock dropped in value from $50 a share to $40 a share. When we sold on Monday, we[6] suffered an even greater loss than we anticipated.

Our financial advisors acted immediately[7] after we asked them to sell the stock; they did not delay. The fault is entirely ours, not theirs.

I am sorry[8] to have to report this news, and I can assure you that in the future there will be no such delay in acting[9] on the wishes of the board. Max Keith [187]

6 Dear Ms. Pulaski: Recently we reviewed your company's checking account, and we are pleased to advise you that[1] effective March 1 your checking charges will be included as part of our new, convenient checking plan for small[2] businesses.

Because you write fewer than 50 checks each month, we are able to provide you with a simpler, more[3] efficient method of check charges. These charges will be based on your closing monthly balance. If you have a[4] minimum balance of $1,000 at the end of the month, you will not be charged for any checks you write. If[5] you have between $500 and $1,000 in your account, you will be charged only $1[6] per month. If you have less than $500, you will be charged $3 for our services.

We would be pleased[7] to answer any questions you might have regarding this new service or about your monthly charges; just call our[8] branch manager, Miss Betty Brown. Our objective is to make your banking easier and less expensive for you.[9] Cordially yours, [183]

7 Dear Mr. Roberts: Your financial records are very important to you and to us. It is essential that[1] our company keep complete and accurate records for you, but we need your help in order to do so.

If you[2] move to a new address or get a new phone number, please be sure to report the change to the records section[3] at our main office as soon as possible. Thank you for helping us keep our records accurate and up to date.[4] Sincerely yours, [83]

LESSON 44

Office-Style Dictation

1 *(As dictated)* Dear Subscriber: There are only ten days left to take advantage of the offer that we made to you last month. (Make that *special offer.)* As you know, we make this offer once every few years.

If you have not already filled out the card (Make that *order card.*) and sent us your check for just $1, we urge you to do so immediately. When we receive your order card and your check, we will send you a list of books from which you may choose four.

For only $1 you get four books that would be worth much more if you were to buy them at a retail outlet. Sincerely yours,

1 *(As it would be transcribed)* Dear Subscriber: There are only ten days left to take advantage of the special offer that we made to you last[1] month. As you know, we make this offer once every few years.

If you have not already filled out the order card and[2] sent us your check for just $1, we urge you to do so immediately. When we receive your order card[3] and your check, we will send you a list of books from which you may choose four.

For only $1 you get four books that[4] would be worth much more if you were to buy them at a retail outlet. Sincerely yours, [95]

3 Gentlemen: A few days ago I read in a financial newspaper about your bond fund. I understand that[1] the fund is exempt from federal, state, and local income taxes. My opinion is that this type of investment[2] would be wise for someone in my tax bracket and for people who do not have any dependents and only[3] a few deductions.

Will you please answer several questions for me. If I were to invest with your organization,[4] could I start by investing no more than $2,000? Is it possible to add to the same account[5] in the future, or would I have to open a new account? Is it possible to liquidate my account[6] should I need cash immediately?

Will you please send me your latest financial report and any other information[7] you have gathered about the tax-exempt bonds. Sincerely yours, [153]

4 Dear Mr. Day: The Municipal Bond Fund is just what I have been waiting for. For the past few years I have been[1] paying extremely high income taxes. I welcome the opportunity to invest without having to pay[2] high taxes on the dividends I receive.

Enclosed are my check for $5,000 and my application[3] form. Will you please send me any necessary forms to sign and the forms I will need to return each time I send[4] an additional payment. Thank you for your assistance, Mr. Day. Sincerely yours, [95]

5 Dear Miss Washington: A few days ago I received a statement of annuity premiums that I paid during[1] the year and an illustration of the annuity income I would receive at retirement under certain[2] stated conditions. Frankly, I am confused by the statement.

I cannot figure out why all the money I[3] invested is not earning the same amount of interest or dividend. It appears that half of my investment[4] is bringing me a much lower return than the other half. Maybe I misunderstood my financial counselor,[5] but I thought all my money would be earning at least 7 percent interest.

I hope you can give me a[6] clarification of the problem. Any answers you can give me will be greatly appreciated. Cordially[7] yours, [141]

6 Dear Miss Stern: I am sorry to say that we seldom take the time to tell our customers that we appreciate[1] their business. The purpose of this note is just to tell you that we do appreciate your maintaining regular[2] checking and savings accounts with the Nashville National Bank. You are a valued depositor and customer,[3] and we want you to know we are grateful for your business.

If you should have need for any special banking service[4] at any time, please do not hesitate to call us. We would be pleased to render any special service that is[5] needed. Yours very truly, [105]

7 Dear Mr. Baker: You have had an account with us for several years. You have made many large purchases from[1] us, and you have al-

ways paid your bills on time. Seldom have we had to wait more than a few days' time for your payments.[2] We are grateful to you for your prompt payments.

Our company is now offering another service to its valued[3] customers. For only 30 cents for each $100 of your current unpaid balance, you can purchase[4] life and disability insurance covering your account balance up to $5,000. It is[5] protection for you if you should suffer total disability; it is protection for your family in[6] the event of your death.

If you are interested in this protection, fill out, sign, and return the enclosed form. The[7] premium will automatically be added to your statement each month. Yours truly, [155]

8 Dear Miss Yates: We are enclosing a supply of envelopes that you can use when you mail your deposits to the[1] City Savings Association. Let us remind you that you should not send cash through the mail under any[2] circumstances. If you want to make deposits by mail, please send either a check or a money order.

When you send[3] your deposit, please enclose your passbook so that we can bring it up to date for you. If you lose your passbook, notify[4] us immediately. Very truly yours, [89]

9 Dear Ms. Barker: Thank you for the copy of *How To Invest Wisely in Mutual Funds* that you gave me when I[1] visited your office last Monday. There is much valuable information about purchasing mutual funds[2] in the *booklet.** Thank you also, Ms. Barker, for answering my specific questions about mutual funds.

I[3] told you last Monday that I would be able to invest at least $10,000 soon. This investment is[4] contingent upon my selling a house in Miami, Florida. It appears that the contract of sale will clear[5] without any *difficulties*† within a week or two. When the contract is signed, I will see you about which mutual[6] funds you would recommend. Yours cordially, [128]

Also correct:
*book, brochure, circular
†problems, trouble

LESSON 45

3 Dear Mr. Simms: Enclosed is your new International credit card. I am sure you will be pleased with it. The[1] International credit card is welcomed by more than 100,000 businesses, airlines, and hotels throughout[2] the world. When you present your International credit card, you are recognized as a person who is financially[3] responsible.

Please read the enclosed credit agreement, Mr. Simms. It outlines our credit terms and explains[4] all charges. When you have had an opportunity to read the agreement, please call our offices should you[5] have any questions.

We know you will enjoy using your new International credit card. Very sincerely[6] yours, [121]

4 Dear Mr. Meyers: On checking my credit records, you will find that I am of sound character, I am reputable,[1] and I am respected. Since I moved to Midland in 1978, I have met many executives[2] of large companies; all of them could serve as personal references for me.

As you probably know,[3] I filed an application with the Interstate Bank for a loan two weeks ago. However, you have not acknowledged[4] receipt of the financial records or the application that I sent. I wonder if you have an answer[5] for me. Have you consented to granting me the loan of $50,000 for the purpose of updating[6] the equipment in my office?

If you need further information, please do not hesitate to contact me at[7] my office. I will supply you with additional financial statements if you wish. I am eager to hear from[8] you. Cordially yours, [164]

5 Dear Investor: We have good news for our investors, and we do not want to wait for the quarterly report to[1] announce it.

During the fourth quarter our board of directors voted to double the dividend on the company's[2] stock. This brings the annual dividend from $2 to $4 a share. This is the highest stock[3] dividend in our history. It reflects our company's strong performance during the year.

In last year's annual[4] report we stated that we entered the year stronger as a company than at any other time in our[5] history. This year's performance makes us even stronger today.

You may expect uninterrupted growth and an even[6] larger return on your stocks next year. Thank you for investing in our company. Cordially yours, [138]

6 Dear Investor: Recently we have received questions from several of our clients regarding how we buy and[1] sell stocks for them. We think all of you might be interested in knowing the procedures that investment firms follow.[2]

You decide you want to buy the stock of a particular firm. You must buy it from a person who currently[3] owns the stock and wants to sell it. An owner who wants to sell stock must sell to an investor who wants to buy it.[4] You realize, of course, it would be almost impossible for you to find someone to buy or sell a particular[5] stock on your own. That is why you come to us, your stockbroker.

You place your order with us, and we in turn place[6] your order with our representative at the stock exchange. The agent approaches the current stockholder's agent[7] to see if a purchase can be made for you. If it can, the transaction takes place. The agent then notifies[8] our representative who notifies us; we then notify you.

We hope this explanation clarifies some[9] of the questions you might have had. If not, please do not hesitate to call us. Yours very truly, [197]

7 Dear Mrs. James: The Miller Investment Company of Los Angeles, California, has added a great number[1] of customers during the past six months; therefore, we are expanding our offices. In order to staff these[2] offices, we will need a number of new, highly efficient people who are interested in making a career of helping others[3] plan their financial futures.

Miss Lydia Gomez, a mutual friend, called to my attention the fact that you[4] might want to return to work. Because you worked for us five years ago, we know you are a capable, reliable[5] person who does excellent work.

If you would like to discuss the matter, please come in to see me. My office[6] is now located at 400 Interstate Parkway, which is near the Jefferson Drive interchange. I hope to[7] see you and to work with you again in the near future. Sincerely yours, [153]

CHAPTER 10

LESSON 46

3 Dear Friend: The Central Credit Association is making a new service available to all residents[1] of the Chicago, Illinois, area. On Monday, January 5, we will open our new counseling[2] office at 482 West 26 Street here in Chicago.

Anyone in the area may come to[3] the office without an appointment and discuss any credit problems with our well-trained, experienced counselors.[4] Our people will give advice free of charge concerning any aspect of credit. We will help people decide[5] when it is advisable to borrow money and when it is not. We will suggest several possible sources[6] of credit that fit each person's particular needs. We will also suggest a repayment schedule that will[7] not place too great a burden on one's budget.

When a person leaves our office, he or she will have a set of[8] principles on which to make sound decisions about borrowing money.

If you or your employees would like to take[9] advantage of this unique service, all you need do is stop by our office between 9 a.m. and 5 p.m.[10] Monday through Friday. Sincerely yours, [207]

4 Dear Miss Underwood: Congratulations on your graduation from Western State College. This represents a milestone[1] in your personal and professional life, and we are sure your family and friends are quite proud of you.

We[2] here at the First National Bank are also very proud of you. We are happy to have been able to be of[3] financial assistance to you during the past four years, and we hope to be able to help you again in the[4] future.

As a special gift we are adding a $1,000 line of credit to your present checking account.[5] If you wish to borrow any amount up to your credit limit, all you need do is write yourself a loan.[6] We will automatically transfer whatever funds are needed to your checking account. You will pay only 8[7] percent interest on the unpaid balance, and you will have up to one year to repay both the principal and the interest.[8] If you do not use the line of credit, you will pay no interest, of course.

Best wishes, Miss Underwood, for a[9] wonderful, successful future. Sincerely yours, [188]

5 Gentlemen: Recently I received my monthly statement from the Acme Gas Company and was astonished to[1] find the total amount due was $187.65. According to my records,[2] all I owe you is $12.65 for one tank of gasoline.

As I checked through the copies of the[3] bills you enclosed, I discovered the principal reason for the error. You enclosed with my statement ten bills that[4] are not mine. These bills belong to a friend of mine, Mr. Frank R. Smith, the principal of an elementary[5] school in my neighborhood. My name is Frank A. Smith. Those bills account for nearly $100; I cannot account[6] for the remainder.

I am enclosing check No. 106 for $12.65 in full payment[7] of my account. I am also enclosing the bills that do not belong to me. Will you please ask your bookkeeper[8] to be more careful in the future. Thank you for taking care of this matter. Yours truly, [177]

6 Dear Miss O'Brien: You may not be happy about having to work while you are going to school, but working is[1] to your advantage. Students who work while going to school are usually more adept at managing their finances[2] after graduation. They have learned the principles of financial responsibility.

When you are working,[3] you must keep complete, accurate records of your weekly and monthly expenditures. You must learn to plan ahead[4] for emergencies. It is definitely in your self-interest to open a savings account and add to[5] it regularly. If you will treat your savings account like a regular expense in your budget, it is easy[6] to save for the future.

To open an account with the Eastern State Bank, just stop by one of our conveniently[7] located offices anytime between 9 a.m. and 5 p.m. Monday through Friday. You will be glad[8] you did. Sincerely yours, [164]

LESSON 47

3 Dear Mr. Jordan: I feel compelled to write this letter to you because I am disturbed by the action recently[1] taken by your bank.

On March 3 I applied in person for two loans that totaled $15,000. One was[2] to be repaid in three years, and the other was to be repaid in two years. I left your office with the[3] understanding that the loans would be approved.

Yesterday, however, I received a letter from the United[4] Mutual Bank telling me that both applications had been refused and that the loans would not be granted. There was no[5] offer of explanation for this action.

It is my contention that I was unjustly turned down for credit,[6] and I want to know why. As you know, the law states that I am entitled to know the reason you refused me credit.[7]

I hope you will look into this matter personally, Mr. Jordan, and let me hear from you soon. Cordially[8] yours, [161]

4 Ladies and Gentlemen: I have always modeled myself after my father because he was an astute manager.[1] When I was a young boy, my father dispelled my notion that there was anything wrong with borrowing money.[2] However, he made sure that I understood that there should be a very good reason for borrowing money.

I[3] now have a teenage son of my own. He will be enrolling in State College this fall, and I definitely have[4] a good reason for borrowing money now. I have projected my budget for the next four years, and I believe[5] that I will need to borrow $10,000 for my son's tuition, books, and living expenses. I hope to[6] be able to repay the loan over a ten-year period after my son's graduation.

Is your bank[7] interested in making educational loans? If it is, please send me the proper application blanks. Thanks for your[8] consideration. Sincerely yours, [164]

5 Dear Mr. Lang: You will recall that several months ago we wrote to you about the overdue balance of[1] your charge account. Our records show that you have owed us $100 since January 2. We have written[2] to you three times, but you have not acknowledged any of our letters.

We know that $100 is not a[3] great deal of money. However, it represents an obligation on your part. If we do not receive your check[4] or at least a letter of explanation within the next week, we will be compelled to close your account and revoke[5] your credit privileges with our organization.

Will you please take this opportunity to write to us,[6] Mr. Lang. We are sure you do not wish to have your credit canceled, and we do not want to lose a customer.[7] Yours truly,

[142]

6 Dear Miss Brooks: Miss Maria Mendez, our credit manager, sent me a memorandum today indicating[1] that you just made the last payment on your home mortgage. Miss Mendez stated that at no time did we send you even[2] a routine reminder and that you made each month's payment promptly. Congratulations on your fine record, Miss Brooks.[3]

We hope you will come to the First National Bank whenever you wish to borrow money in the future. We[4] will be very glad to see you. Sincerely yours,

PS. Your canceled mortgage is enclosed. [96]

7 Dear Mr. Young: Have you ever made a loan to someone who did not repay you when the money was due? You have[1] not repaid the money that you borrowed from us six months ago. You promised us that the principal and interest,[2] which totaled $1,000, would be in our hands within four months.

You are a business executive and must[3] realize that it is necessary to collect outstanding debts. If your customers do not pay their bills in[4] accordance with your credit terms, you probably must borrow money in order to pay your own debts. This, of course,[5] imposes an unfair financial burden on you.

We are bearing an unfair financial burden because we have[6] not received your payment. Please send us your check for $1,000 soon so that we will not have to turn this matter[7] over to our attorneys. Sincerely yours, [149]

LESSON 48

3 Gentlemen: On a recent visit to St. Louis, Missouri, I stayed at the International Hotel. When[1] I was leaving the hotel on February 12, I presented my General credit card to the clerk.

The[2] clerk told me that the hotel would not take my General card in payment of my bill; however, the hotel would[3] honor either the National card or the Continental card. I had neither a National card nor a[4] Continental card; therefore, I had to pay cash. Unfortunately, this was not the first time that my General credit[5] card had been refused by a major hotel. It was the last time, however.

Enclosed is my card; please close my[6] account. Yours truly, [124]

4 Gentlemen: In January I will be leaving for England and Spain. I will be gone for at least six months, and[1] I am concerned about how to handle my finances on the trip. I suppose that I should take either traveler's[2] checks or regular bank checks with me.

Will you please let me have your opinion about what I should do. Thank you[3] for your help. Sincerely yours, [65]

5 To the Staff: As you probably know, our company has made arrangements for you to get reduced rates when you rent[1] cars for company business. Now we are pleased to announce that you can enjoy the same discount when you rent cars for[2] your personal use.

Attached is a discount card that will enable you to get a reduced rate at any of[3] the five largest rental companies. Be sure to take your discount card with you when you travel. You will need neither[4] further identification nor extra cash to rent a car. Fred Smith [93]

6 Dear Mr. Roberts: Now that the price of a new boat is so low, shouldn't you consider buying a new boat? Drive[1] out to the Lake of the Woods today, and choose the boat you would like to own.

The sailboats, motorboats, and yachts are so[2] well constructed that you will delight in bringing your family to the lake and taking them for boat rides. This summer[3] the fishing has been at its best, and the sunshine has been abundant. We know you will enjoy this new way of[4] life.

Our terms are easy and convenient, and our interest rates are exceedingly low. Bring your family to the[5] Lake of the Woods to see the boat of your dreams. Yours truly, [110]

7 To the Staff: Sometimes we should send a note of thanks to our special charge customers. A survey that we made less than[1] six months ago showed that most of our charge customers have had their charge cards for more than five years. It also showed they[2] have been paying their bills promptly.

We must bring to the attention of these special customers the fact that we[3] appreciate their business. We must take them seriously and keep them coming to our store for many more years.

Please[4] send a note of appreciation to each of the special charge customers assigned to you. Your list is enclosed.[5] Jack Rhodes [101]

8 Dear Ms. O'Brien: We are enclosing the following items that you requested:

1. A copy of our[1] financial statement as of December 31.
2. A list of the suppliers with whom we have done business during[2] the past five years and those who have extended us credit privileges.
3. A list of the banks in which we have[3] accounts.

If there is any other information you need in order to initiate our line of credit,[4] we would be happy to either take or send it to you. Yours truly, [93]

LESSON 49

Office-Style Dictation

1 *(As dictated)* Mr. Day: On January 30 we will have our annual review of the financial condition of our company. In preparation for this review, I would like you to obtain the following statistics:

1. The number of active accounts that we have.
2. The total amount due us as of December 31.
3. The total interest and principal we received during the past year.

Please have your preliminary report to me by January 15. Jane Smith (Let's add another item to the list: *4. The number and amounts of uncollectible accounts on our books.)*

1 *(As it would be transcribed)* Mr. Day: On January 30 we will have our annual review of the financial condition of[1] our company. In preparation for this review, I would like you to obtain the following statistics:

1.[2] The number of active accounts that we have.
2. The total amount due us as of December 31.
3.[3] The total interest and principal we received during the past year.
4. The number and amounts of uncollectible[4] accounts on our books.

Please have your preliminary report to me by January 15. Jane Smith[5] [100]

3 Dear Mr. Simmons: Would you like to have a bank credit card from the United Bank? Thousands of people are now[1] enjoying the convenience of this valuable card.

Let us reassure you that it is not difficult to obtain[2] a credit card from the United Bank. Enclosed is the short application form that is required. All you need[3] to do is fill out the form and then either bring it to the bank or mail it to us. We will then verify the[4] information you have included on it.

The application is neither long nor complicated; it is[5] actually quite simple. We ask questions about only the following three items: your current job status, your monthly[6] income, and your total debts. No question is difficult to answer, and all your answers will be kept in strict[7] confidence.

Take a few minutes today, Mr. Simmons, to complete, sign, and return the form to us. Cordially[8] yours, [161]

4 Dear Mrs. Smith: I read in the Wednesday, February 3, issue of the *Troy Journal* that you plan to open[1] a new furniture store in the Village Mall Shopping Center at 703 26th Street. Congratulations,[2] Mrs. Smith; we are sure you will be very successful in this new, exciting venture.

We here at the Eastern[3] National Bank stand ready to help you in any way possible. If you want to remodel the store that[4] you will occupy, we will help you with the financing. If you want to obtain a loan to finance your inventory,[5] we will be very happy to work with you. If you want to finance your accounts receivable, we can[6] easily assist you.

In short, we are ready to help you with all your financial needs. Just stop by our bank at[7] any time during regular banking hours; one of our well-trained, experienced representatives will be happy[8] to assist you. Very cordially yours, [168]

5 Dear Ms. Davis: We know how busy you are as a manager of a large apartment complex. We also know[1] how much time you spend processing the applications submitted by prospective tenants. Let us take some of the[2] burden off your shoulders so that you can have more time for your other, more important responsibilities.

The[3] Boston Credit Bureau does expert processing of tenant applications. We can prepare commercial credit[4] reports and furnish you with the credit background of prospective tenants. We have the means of completing rudimentary[5] checks that may be difficult for managers of apartment complexes to do themselves.

If you are interested[6] in learning more about our services, please fill out, sign, and return the enclosed card. We will contact you shortly[7] after we receive the card. Yours truly, [148]

6 Dear Mr. Tate: Have you ever gone shopping and found that you did not have enough *cash** to pay for the items that[1] you wanted to purchase? If you have, you know that this situation can cause you a great deal of inconvenience[2] and embarrassment.

We can help you to prevent this kind of thing from happening. The Jennings credit card is yours[3] for the asking. All you need do to *obtain*† one is fill out the enclosed form and mail it to us in the[4] envelope that is provided.

Don't wait until you are in an embarrassing, inconvenient situation;

order[5] your card today. Sincerely yours, [107]

Also correct:

*money

†get

LESSON 50

3 Dear Customer: With the large number of credit options available these days, it is important that everyone[1] understand fully the various aspects of credit financing. The Mutual Bank of Cleveland is[2] publishing a new, completely revised edition of its enlightening booklet, *Understanding Credit.* In this booklet[3] you will find answers to a multitude of questions concerning credit. Included are such topics as the[4] following:

1. When it is advisable to borrow.
2. How a person can estimate the cost of a loan.[5]
3. What credit sources are available for various types of purchases.

If you would like to have a copy[6] of *Understanding Credit,* just sign and return the enclosed self-addressed card. When we receive it, we will send[7] your booklet to you by return mail. Yours truly, [149]

4 Dear Friend: When you save at the Central Savings and Loan Association, you can watch your savings multiply every[1] day. Yes, we actually figure the interest on your savings account every day of the year. Interest is[2] compounded daily, and you can see your savings increase on a day-to-day basis.

In this day of ever-increasing[3] inflation and high taxes, it just doesn't make sense to let your extra cash sit idle in a regular[4] checking account when it could be accumulating interest every day.

If you would like to have more information[5] about the various savings plans offered by Central Savings and Loan, just write or call us; we will be happy[6] to help you. Sincerely yours, [126]

5 Mrs. Pryor: As you know, for the past several years our accounts receivable have been increasing at a[1] very fast pace. Just three years ago our accounts receivable amounted to approximately[2] $100,000. Today, however, the figure has grown to more than $250,000.

If our[3] sales had increased proportionately, I would have little concern about this matter. However, our sales have[4] actually decreased. To make matters worse, I find that almost 10 percent of our accounts are more than a month past due.[5] More than 5 percent are at least six months past due.

It should be obvious to everyone that our company is[6] facing a multitude of problems, and these problems must be solved in the immediate future. If we do not[7] find satisfactory solutions, we will be out of business within a year's time. J. D. Norris [158]

6 Dear Mr. Jefferson: On Monday, the 21st of April, you ordered 25 bolts of multicolored[1] fabric from the Atlas Department Store. At that time you agreed to pay for the goods when they were delivered in[2] satisfactory condition to your store at

1407 32d Street in Elgin, Illinois.[3]

On June 5 the goods were delivered to your warehouse, and the person at your receiving dock accepted them. A[4] bill for $2,000 was enclosed with the order. At the end of June we had not received your payment for[5] the material, and we mailed you a duplicate bill. Still another month has passed, and you have not even[6] acknowledged our two statements.

Frankly, Mr. Jefferson, we went to a great deal of effort and expense to manufacture[7] the material to your specifications. We did this because you had been a good customer of[8] ours for a period of more than ten years. We invested our own money; we did not even ask you for a[9] deposit.

Now we are faced with the unpleasant prospect of having to turn your account over to our attorneys[10] for collection. Please do not make us take this action. It will do neither of us any good. We will lose a[11] customer, and you will probably lose your good credit rating. Please send us your check for $2,000 by[12] return mail, or at least acknowledge this letter. Yours truly, [251]

7 Dear Mr. Drake: It is quite easy to lose a letter. Every day each of us receives a multitude of letters.[1] Some of them are important; others are not. Perhaps you lost the friendly reminder that we mailed to you last[2] month. Our letter stated that your payment of $1,000 on your account was overdue.

If you lost the[3] letter, will you please take a moment now to write us a check. If there is some other reason why we have not received[4] your check, we would like to know about it. Please let us hear from you within a few days' time, Mr. Drake. Sincerely[5] yours, [101]

CHAPTER 11

LESSON 51

3 Dear Friend: Is your money going up the chimney this winter? Unfortunately, this is happening in many[1] homes. Homeowners are paying hundreds of dollars to heat their homes. However, a great deal of the heated air is[2] lost because there is nothing to stop it from escaping through the chimney when the furnace is not working.

The Fuel[3] Saver, a new device designed to save you as much as 30 percent on your heating bills, is now available[4] exclusively from Jennings Associates. This unique device is patented and registered with the[5] United States government.

One of our factory-trained, experienced people can come to your home and install a[6] Fuel Saver in a matter of only a few hours' time. A special valve will open when your furnace is operating[7] and close when it is off. The heat and your hard-earned money will not escape through the open chimney.

You can[8] have a Fuel Saver for only a few cents a day. During the winter you could save hundreds of dollars. Doesn't[9] it make sense to call us today? Our telephone number is 555-8090. Sincerely yours, [198]

4 Dear Mr. Taylor: Three weeks ago your company installed a new device in my gas-burning furnace. The device[1] was designed to decrease the loss of heat when the furnace was not operating.

For the first two weeks it[2] operated satisfactorily; I could hear the valve closing intermittently. About a week ago,[3] however, I stopped hearing the valve opening and closing. In addition, I occasionally smelled the strong scent[4] of natural gas throughout my house. When I first noticed the scent, I called your offices. One of your people told me[5] that there was probably nothing wrong with the system and that I should call the gas company.

A representative[6] of the gas company came to my house. After a short investigation, the representative said: "I[7] am afraid that you have spent a great deal of money on a worthless item. It doesn't work properly, and I[8] had to disconnect it in order to prevent gas from escaping."

Under the circumstances, Mr. Taylor,[9] I must insist that I receive a full refund of the $1,000 I paid your company. I will expect[10] to hear from you soon. Yours truly,

PS. I will also expect reimbursement for the $20 charge[11] I had to pay the gas company. [227]

5 Dear Miss Morris: Many years ago people kept their life's savings hidden away in their homes. Money was often[1] placed in the back of a closet or under a mattress. This sounds ludicrous, of course, because the money was not[2] earning interest, and it certainly was not safe.

Did you know that today many people are taking similar[3] risks with their money? Money kept in a regular checking account does not earn interest; it is actually working[4] no harder than money hidden away in a closet. Because of inflation today, every dollar kept[5] in a regular checking account will probably be worth no more than 90 cents in actual purchasing[6] power in a year's time.

Some people try to protect their money from inflation by investing in unsound[7] financial schemes that promise extremely high yields. Unfortunately, they sometimes lose every cent that they have. Their money[8] was actually no safer than money hidden under a mattress.

Is there a way you can protect your money[9] and receive a guaranteed return? There is one way; you can invest in government bonds. Government bonds pay[10] a fixed dividend, and they are tax-exempt. To learn more about how you can protect your savings and keep your money[11] working at the same time, just return the self-addressed card. We will be glad to send you more information.[12] Sincerely yours,

[242]

LESSON 52

3 Dear Mrs. Ray: One thousand copies of the first printing of the highly publicized new book, *The Challenge of Running,*[1] have been allotted to us for our regular customers. Our supply will arrive at our bookstore by[2] November 15.

Thousands of people throughout the world have benefited greatly by establishing and following[3] a regular running program. *The Challenge of Running,* which was written by the renowned medical authority,[4] Dr. Jane Bates, should enable thousands more to start benefiting from a well-planned running program.

Enclosed[5] is a circular that describes all the features of this exciting new book. If you would like to reserve a[6] copy, just detach the coupon at the bottom of the circular, fill it out, and return it to us. Your copy[7] of *The Challenge of Running* will be awaiting you at our store after November 15. Very cordially[8] yours, [161]

4 Ladies and Gentlemen: In August I will be transferred to Virginia, and my family and I will need a house in Richmond[1] or in one of its suburbs. Your realty firm has been recommended to me by one of the officers[2] of the Second National Bank here in Omaha, Nebraska. Therefore, I am soliciting your assistance[3] in this matter.

We will need a house with three bedrooms, a living room, two full baths, and a large kitchen. We will also[4] need an attached two-car garage and a large fenced yard.

We hope to be able to buy a suitable house for[5] $90,000. However, we will not be limited to that figure if you can find a house that suits[6] all our needs.

Will you please check the houses that are available and let us know if you have anything that you[7] feel would be suitable. We can fly to Richmond on any weekend during the next month or so to look at any[8] properties you recommend. Very truly yours, [170]

5 Gentlemen: On January 2 I received a leather sports jacket that I had ordered from your company.[1] I was quite disappointed to find that the jacket was not the exact color of the illustration in your[2] catalog. In addition, the quality of the jacket was not as good as I had expected it to be.[3] I definitely feel that the jacket was misrepresented in your catalog.

Under the circumstances,[4] I am returning the jacket to you; you should receive it in a day or so. Please adjust the balance of my[5] account by crediting it for the purchase price of the jacket and the shipping charges. Yours truly, [118]

6 Gentlemen: In your advertisement in the June issue of *Automotive Repair,* you mentioned that retailers[1] were welcome to send for a free catalog of automobile parts and accessories. Will you please send me a[2] copy.

I recently purchased an automobile parts store in Trenton, New Jersey, and am now in the process[3] of stocking my shelves. I am particularly interested in stocking the repair kits that have permitted novice[4] mechanics to complete simple repairs successfully.

If you have any additional information[5] that might be of benefit to me, I would appreciate receiving it too. I am starting my business on[6] a limited budget, and I am looking for savings on all my purchases. Very truly yours, [138]

7 Dear Mrs. Davis: We are pleased to announce that the Edwards Card Shop has been completely remodeled and will[1] reopen on Monday, March 21.

In our beautifully decorated store, which is located at 402[2] Main Drive, we have everything from greeting cards to monogrammed stationery. In addition, we have an enlarged[3] gift shop where you will be able to find unique gifts from various countries throughout the world.

Please plan to come[4] in on March 21 and help us celebrate our reopening. We will be looking forward to seeing you.[5] Sincerely yours, [103]

LESSON 53

3 Dear Mr. Cummings: The Smith Department Store would like to do something special for you to show you how much we[1] appreciate your business. We feel that it is only right that we do something very special for our charge customers.[2] Therefore, we will conduct a sale next Monday, June 4, from 6 p.m. until 9 p.m. in our main store at[3] 816 Tenth Avenue.

The only persons who will be allowed to pass through our doors are our special charge[4] customers who bring their invitations with them. Your invitation is enclosed with this letter.

During this special[5] three-hour sale you will be able to make substantial savings on every item in our store. Some things will be reduced[6] as much as 50 percent.

Don't you think you should be here when we open our doors, Mr. Cummings? We look forward[7] to serving you. Sincerely yours, [147]

4 Dear Miss Wild: Three weeks ago I was in your wholesale store and placed a rather large order for towels. I wanted to[1] sell them in my retail store here in Erie, Pennsylvania. All the towels that I selected were in stock at the[2] time, and your sales representative assured me that they would be delivered promptly. I expected them to be[3] delivered within a week's time.

I finally received a box from your company today. Unfortunately,[4] the towels that you sent to me are not the right ones. I ordered light green and yellow towels; you sent dark blue ones. I ordered[5] 100 towels; you sent 200.

Frankly, I am chagrined. I have been purchasing items in your store for[6] many years, and I have usually received first-class service. During the past year, however, I have not received[7] the type of service I feel I deserve. Based on the type of service you have given me recently, I will have[8] to take my business elsewhere. The towels are being returned to you separately. Yours truly, [176]

5 Dear Mr. Trent: Because you are a stamp collector, the National Philatelic Society would like to[1] issue you a special invitation to become a member of our unique organization.

We are sure[2] you have heard of the

many services that our organization provides to its members. For the low yearly[3] membership fee of $25, you will receive a copy of our nationally recognized magazine,[4] *Stamp Collecting*. Each issue of the magazine contains interesting, fact-filled articles about the various[5] phases of stamp collecting.

When you are a member of our organization, you will have the opportunity[6] to purchase newly issued stamps from countries throughout the world. They will be available to you at their[7] initial face value. However, as our long-time members know, many of the stamps quickly increase in value.[8] We do not guarantee that all stamps will increase in value, but many do.

Because of your interest in collecting[9] stamps, we believe that you will agree you definitely should be a member of the National Philatelic[10] Society. To become a member, all you need do is fill out the enclosed application blank, attach[11] your check for $25, and mail both to us in the envelope that is provided. Cordially yours, [239]

6 Dear Friend: Now that winter is almost over, I am sure you are thinking about getting your garden and yard into[1] top condition.

Cunningham Garden Shops have everything you will need to get your garden and yard ready for[2] the spring, summer, and autumn months.

We have several kinds of grass seed that are especially designed for areas[3] that receive a great deal of light or for areas that are shaded. We have flowers already in bloom that[4] can be planted in your garden. In addition, we have every kind of garden tool that you will need.

Don't you think[5] you ought to pay us a visit soon? There is a conveniently located Cunningham Garden Shop at[6] 2107 West 21 Street. We hope to see you soon. Sincerely yours, [134]

LESSON 54

Office-Style Dictation

1 *(As dictated)* Mr. Becker: It has been called to my attention that sales have been declining for the past three months. As you know, it is absolutely (Underscore *absolutely.*) necessary that we meet our sales goal if we are going to make a profit.

Please call a meeting of all members (Put *all members* in capital letters.) of your staff for next Monday morning at 9 a.m. I will meet with you in the conference room to discuss our plans for the rest of the year. Naturally, everyone should be prepared to participate in the discussion.

If you have any suggestions, I would appreciate receiving them before the meeting. My door is always (Put *always* in all caps.) open. James Davis

1 *(As it would be transcribed)* Mr. Becker: It has been called to my attention that sales have been declining for the past three months. As you know,[1] it is <u>absolutely</u> necessary that we meet our sales goal if we are going to make a profit.

Please call[2] a meeting of ALL

MEMBERS of your staff for next Monday morning at 9 a.m. I will meet with you in the[3] conference room to discuss our plans for the rest of the year. Naturally, everyone should be prepared to participate[4] in the discussion.

If you have any suggestions, I would appreciate receiving them before the meeting.[5] My door is ALWAYS open. James Davis [108]

3 Dear Mrs. Jennings: On June 15 we ordered 24 sets of luggage from your store for resale. After[1] receiving your acknowledgment, we expected to have the shipment by July 31 at the latest. On July[2] 25 we received your statement for the total amount due.

It is now August 15, and we still have[3] not received the luggage. In addition, we have not received an answer to any of the letters we mailed to[4] your company. Frankly, I am dismayed.

We plan to advertise the luggage for our annual Labor Day sale.[5] Will you please check into this matter personally, Mrs. Jennings, to see what has happened to our order.

If[6] you cannot get the order to us by the 25th of August, cancel the entire order. Yours truly, [139]

4 Dear Mr. Miles: A special book has just been published for the independent business executive who wants to[1] have the latest information on reducing income taxes.

Professor A. C. Arnold of Phoenix College[2] has written the book, *How To Decrease Your Taxes.* It is especially designed to bring the independent business[3] executive up to date on the latest federal legislation. The book includes many facts in an[4] easy-to-read format. The cost of this book is only $8.95.

We invite you to examine[5] the book for ten days at no charge; merely return the enclosed form in the self-addressed envelope that is enclosed.[6] If you are not satisfied with the book, return it to us; you will owe us nothing. If you decide that you[7] want to keep the book, just send us your check. Cordially yours, [150]

5 Dear Ms. Patterson: What would your family do if you were to die suddenly? Would they be able to live[1] in the same manner to which they are accustomed? Would they be able to keep their present home? Would your children be[2] able to continue attending the same school in the same neighborhood? They will be able to do all these things[3] if you have sufficient life insurance. Unfortunately, many people do not plan properly for this[4] contingency. If the breadwinner dies, the spouse is faced with severe financial problems.

If you have not taken care[5] of this vital matter, now is the time to take positive action. You can provide all the protection your[6] family would need if you should die. This protection costs only a small amount, and it can be paid monthly, quarterly,[7] or annually.

For more information, just return the enclosed card today; we will send one of our well-trained,[8] experienced representatives to discuss the matter with you. Very sincerely yours, [177]

6 To the Sales Staff: Congratulations on the excellent work you have been doing in selling our new and used cars.[1] I have just reviewed the sales figures for the first six months of this year, and I am pleased to report that our sales have increased[2] by 20 percent over the corresponding period last year. If our sales budget for the remainder[3] of the year is met, our financial picture will be very bright indeed.

Keep up the good work. Fred Mendez [78]

7 Dear Mrs. Wyatt: Everyone wants to save money these days. We are offering you a special way to do so.[1] For a limited time only, you can subscribe to our magazine, *Making and Keeping Money,* for about half[2] the newsstand price.

By reading the interesting articles in this magazine, you can do the following:

1. Save[3] up to 60 percent of the price of your next airline ticket.
2. Cut your home heating bills by as much as 50[4] percent.
3. Lower your local, state, and federal income taxes.

To take advantage of our unique offer,[5] it is essential that you act quickly. Just fill in the accompanying *form** and return it to us[6] immediately. Within two weeks' time you will be reading the informative articles and saving *substantial*†[7] sums of money.

The offer is good only during the month of July; order your subscription today. Let us[8] help you save money. Sincerely yours, [167]

Also correct:
*blank
†large, great

LESSON 55

3 Dear Ms. Webster: Thank you for requesting that we print your early spring catalog. During the past few years, we have[1] enjoyed printing many of your sales brochures; therefore, we know how important your catalog is and how much your[2] customers rely on it. Our experienced printers will plan your catalog with care and attention.

In your[3] letter you requested that we print the catalog in three colors and use a specific paper. We have this[4] paper in stock, but using this weight of paper will give you a very bulky, heavy catalog. The weight of[5] this paper will, therefore, add significantly to the cost of postage.

We suggest that you consider a lighter[6] paper. We have enclosed samples of several weights of paper that we think would be better for your catalog.[7] Each of them is actually less expensive than your original choice of paper.

We will wait until we[8] hear from you before we proceed with the work, of course. Sincerely yours, [172]

4 Dear Mr. Shelton: My buyers and I are planning to be in Tucson, Arizona, next month for the regional[1] fashion shows for women's and children's clothing. We are wondering if you will be displaying your new spring fashions[2] sometime during that month.

Our sales were much higher this year than they were last year, and we attribute the increase[3] to the fact that we carried more of your lightweight designer clothes than we had in the past. Your styles and colors[4] certainly help entice our customers to buy new garments.

We hope you are planning to present your spring line during[5] the month we are in Tucson. Cordially yours, [108]

5 Gentlemen: Recently I purchased a Master lawn mower from the Master Service Company in Toledo,[1] Ohio. All the consumer guides I checked stated that the Master was one of the finest, most efficient mowers[2] on the market and that it would give me years of uninterrupted service.

I am unhappy to report[3] to you that I have had my mower for only three months and have had a great deal of trouble with it. It is[4] extremely difficult to start, and I have to wait three or four minutes after it is running before I can begin[5] using the machine. If I do not, the motor stops running. I have taken the mower back to the service[6] center several times during these three months, but I have not received satisfactory service.

Under the[7] circumstances, I feel that I should receive a new mower. Do you agree? I am anxiously awaiting your reply.[8] Cordially yours, [164]

6 Mr. Poland: Congratulations on your promotion. All of us in the main office here in Flint, Michigan,[1] wish you success as our new director of marketing. We are looking forward to working with you in your new[2] position.

As you know, the company will pay a reputable moving company the cost of moving your[3] household furniture and furnishings to Flint. In addition, we will assist you in selling your present home in[4] Mobile. In order to do so, however, you must obtain three appraisals of the value of your property.[5] The average of the three will be used to establish the minimum selling price. We will guarantee you that you[6] will not have to accept less than this price. However, the selling price could be much higher.

If you need further[7] information, please contact me anytime. Roy Hamilton [150]

7 Dear Miss Rivers: What do you plan to do when you graduate in June? If you are not planning to go to graduate[1] school, perhaps you should think about a career in marketing with Ruiz and Associates.

The profile charts[2] that your college counselor filled out show that you are an eloquent speaker and a good listener, that you like[3] to work with people, and that you have a very nice appearance. These are the traits usually associated[4] with successful marketing representatives.

To find out if a marketing career with Ruiz and Associates[5] is for you, come to our office at 7624 Main Street and talk with one of our personnel[6] counselors. Don't wait; call

555-8206 for an appointment. We look forward to hearing from you.[7] Sincerely yours, [143]

8 To the Staff: All of us should have a good health insurance plan, a comprehensive policy that will help you pay[1] for the cost of medical and surgical care. To obtain a plan that will be low in cost and yet will pay you[2] for most of the expenses incurred for hospital and medical care, we have applied for a group plan that will[3] cover all our employees and their families.

Even if you are already covered by a private plan, we[4] urge you to read the enclosed brochure that outlines our new plan and to compare its coverage and its cost with yours.[5] You may find that by joining our plan you will save a substantial amount of money and still have the same coverage[6] that you now enjoy.

If you join this group by Friday, January 31, you will not have to have a[7] medical examination. Don't wait; fill out the attached application form and return it to us in the[8] envelope that we have provided for this purpose. A. L. Robinson [173]

9 Dear Mr. and Mrs. Worth: Since we received your request last Thursday, we have toured many one-family homes. We[1] looked at a number of four-bedroom brick houses that are for sale. Most of these homes have two full baths; a few have three.[2] A complete description of each house is enclosed.

Please call us next week to tell us which homes you would like to see. We[3] will wait until we hear from you before we go ahead with any further work. Sincerely yours, [77]

CHAPTER 12

LESSON 56

3 Dear Dr. Baker: The alumni association of Bennington College is happy to announce formally[1] its annual trip for graduates. This year we will visit the West Indies. We will depart via steamship[2] from Portland, Maine, on January 28 and return on February 15. As you have formerly[3] enjoyed our other tours, we thought you might be interested in joining us on our cruise this year.

For years ships sailed to[4] the West Indies on the same route. However, our itinerary will be quite different. We will see islands[5] that are unspoiled and seldom visited.

While you are on board ship, you will enjoy a life of comfort and leisure.[6] In the daytime you will relax in the sun or swim in the ship's pool. In the evenings you will enjoy exotic,[7] delicious foods in the elegance of the ship's main dining room.

Send in the enclosed reservation card today[8] to guarantee space for you on this cruise. Very cordially yours, [172]

4 Dear Miss Costello: Many people take vacations to interesting, exciting countries throughout the world, but they[1] really do not gain much from their investment in time and money. They see the usual historic points of interest,[2] of course, but they do not truly understand the people or the countries they visit.

On the other hand, some[3] people spend months reading about the countries they plan to visit. They do this in order to learn about the[4] language, the culture, and the history of the various countries they want to visit. Some people study for[5] years in order to learn more about their own ancestry before visiting a foreign country.

We are happy[6] to announce formally that Eastern State College is instituting a new series of courses this term. These courses[7] are especially designed for international travelers who want to learn more about the countries they[8] plan to visit.

In September we are offering courses in the history and culture of France, Germany,[9] and Spain. If you are planning a European vacation this year, you should definitely take one of these short[10] courses. You will learn in only a few weeks' time what might formerly have taken you many months of individual[11] study.

For more information, just write the registrar of Eastern State College. Sincerely yours, [239]

5 Dear Miss Jenkins: It was formerly believed that taking a vacation was a luxury. Nothing could be further[1] from the truth. Taking a vacation is not a luxury; it is a necessity. Getting away from[2] one's regular routine is essential for good physical and mental health.

Taking the right vacation does not[3] necessarily mean flying to a resort or taking an around-the-world trip. The proper vacation depends[4] strictly on the individual involved. A person who works at a desk eight hours a day may find that a[5] short trip to the seashore will provide just the right change of pace. A person who is involved in vigorous physical[6] activity on a day-to-day basis may find that relaxing at home is "just what the doctor ordered."[7]

To learn more about how to plan your next vacation, write for our brochure, *The Right Vacation for You*. It is yours[8] free of charge. Sincerely yours, [165]

6 Dear Customer: The Southern Travel Service is pleased to announce formally the grand opening of our new[1] offices at 10103 State Street here in Houston, Texas. The Southern Travel Service, which was formerly[2] located at 605 Davis Drive, will continue to offer the wide variety of services that[3] we have always provided our customers. In our new, expanded offices, however, we will be able[4] to serve your needs even better.

We will be able to make hotel and airline reservations through the use of[5] our new computer. We will be able to reserve tickets for dramas, for musical productions, and for sporting[6] events in a matter of only a few minutes' time. In short, we can handle all your travel plans with[7] dependability and efficiency.

Stop by our new offices the next time you are in the area; we[8] will be very happy to see you. Sincerely yours, [169]

7 Dear Friend: Recently Central Airlines conducted a formal survey of its passengers, and we thought you might be[1] interested in the results. We asked our passengers what services they would like us to add to make their business[2] trips more enjoyable. What we learned came as somewhat of a surprise to us.

Our business passengers did not ask[3] for a wide variety of foods. They did not ask for free movies or stereo music. Instead, they asked for[4] a quiet section in each of our planes in which they could read or work without interruption.

Beginning July[5] 1, therefore, we are instituting a new program. We will have a special section on many of our planes; it[6] will be the "executive section." This section will be in the front of the main cabin, and we will make sure that[7] those who sit there will not be disturbed. When the plane is almost filled to capacity, we will see that the empty[8] seats are in the "executive section."

We hope you will take advantage of this special service the next time you[9] have occasion to fly to any of the cities that we serve. When you make your reservation, just specify[10] that you want to be seated in the "executive section." Sincerely yours, [214]

LESSON 57

3 Dear Mr. Smith: Now that summer is almost here, you are probably thinking about your vacation plans. If you[1] are like most business executives, however, you do not have time to take care of the myriad of details[2] involved in vacation planning yourself. Why not let Atlas Travel Service make your plans for you this year.

We can[3] make air, train, and bus reservations in any area in the world. We can also make reservations for[4] you in more than 5,000 hotels and motels throughout the United States and in 25 foreign countries.[5] In addition, we can arrange to have a rental car awaiting your arrival at almost any location.[6]

When you let Atlas Travel Service plan your vacation for you, you will receive substantial discounts on[7] everything from transportation to trinkets. If you wish, we will have payment deferred until six months after you return.[8]

Doesn't it make good sense, Mr. Smith, to let our organization make your vacation plans for you this year?[9] Sincerely yours, [183]

4 Dear Mrs. Cunningham: Two years ago Animal Kingdom opened its vast park to the public. Since then our park[1] has received critical acclaim and is recognized as one of the most unusual, educational parks[2] in the world.

At Animal Kingdom you and your family have the opportunity to see more than 1,000[3] animals from almost every part of the world. You can see lions from Africa and tigers from India.[4] You can see elephants and camels and monkeys. What is more, you can see them in their natural habitat.[5] When you visit our park, you can drive your car through our simulated jungle, or you can take a ride in one of[6] our private, air-conditioned buses.

For a limited time only, we are offering family memberships[7] that are good for the entire summer at substantial savings. If you purchase your family membership before[8] June 1, you will pay only $30. For this small investment you and your family will be able to[9] spend many delightful hours in the park during the next few months.

If you want to take advantage of this unique[10] opportunity, just send us your check today; you will receive your family membership card in the mail within[11] a week's time. Sincerely yours, [226]

5 Dear Mr. and Mrs. Gray: Old West City is a frontier resort that recreates the charm and traditions of[1] a bygone era. It is an internationally known attraction that is also the gateway to the great[2] national parks in Colorado, Wyoming, and Utah.

Old West City is a complete vacation resort.[3] Here you can take all-day horseback trips, explore the wilderness on foot, or take an exciting trip down the river[4] in a canoe. The choice is yours.

In addition to the natural scenic attractions, there are museums, theaters,[5] and a wide variety of restaurants and shops. In short, Old West City is just the place for your family's[6] vacation this year.

The enclosed brochure gives complete details and contains actual photographs. When you read[7] it, you will know why Old West City was preferred last year by more families than any other similar[8] attraction in the West. Sincerely yours, [167]

6 Ladies and Gentlemen: We understand that your organization is planning a regional convention in[1] our area next autumn. If you would like to have your convention in a first-class convention center for a[2] minimum cost, you should consider the George Washington Hotel.

When you have a convention at the George Washington[3] Hotel, you will find that we are as interested in the success of your convention as you are. You will find[4] that our employees are friendly and reliable.

Our conference rooms will hold 3,000 people, and our banquet[5] rooms will accommodate 2,500 people.

If you would like to have more information, please contact[6] our convention director, Ms. Mary McCall, at (272) 555-6161. She will be glad[7] to quote you the special rates that we are offering to all organizations that hold conventions at our hotel[8] during the coming year. Sincerely yours, [168]

LESSON 58

3 Dear Mr. Worth: The Portland Chamber of Commerce is holding an open meeting at Town Hall to discuss changes[1] in routes for our bus system. The meeting will be held in Room 1201 at 7 p.m. on Friday, July[2] 17.

It is our feeling that we should provide expanded bus service to the residents in the suburbs[3] north and east of the city. We hope to offer bus service every ten minutes between the hours of 7[4] and 9 a.m. and between the hours of 4 and 6 p.m. Monday through Friday. These areas are densely[5] populated and definitely need more bus service. The southern and western suburban areas have fewer[6] people and there seems to be no justification for increasing bus service there at this time.

We have already[7] received a number of suggestions from people who live in the affected areas. If you have any[8] suggestions to make, please be prepared to make a short presentation at the meeting; we will be glad to know your[9] feelings about this matter. Sincerely yours, [188]

4 Dear Mr. Cummings: Perhaps you have had the unpleasant experience of driving a great distance, pulling up[1] to a motel, and finding that it was already filled. This will not happen to you when you plan to stay at[2] Lexington Motels.

We have more than 15,000 first-quality motels in cities throughout the United States.[3] Before you begin your next trip, just call (800) 555-5016. One of our courteous, efficient[4] reservations clerks will be glad to guarantee your reservation at one of our conveniently located[5] motels.

When you arrive, you will find that our staff is all ready for you. We will have a clean, comfortable[6] room waiting for you. We will have a delicious meal available if you are hungry. We will even arrange[7] to have your clothes cleaned and waiting for you the following morning.

If you should find that you will not be able to[8] reach your destination, all you need do is call the above number and cancel the reservation. The clerk will[9] be happy to suggest a closer, more convenient location to you.

Don't start out on your next trip without first[10] calling Lexington; you will be making a wise move. Sincerely yours, [213]

5 Dear Jim: Janet and I will never forget the wonderful vacation we had on your boat in June. We had not[1] realized that a few days on the water could be so enjoyable.

Thanks for making the trip so much fun and for[2] inviting us to go with you and Betty again in August. We will be all ready to go when the day arrives.[3] You are certainly wonderful, gracious people.

Please let us know, Jim, if you will be able to spend a few[4] days with us over the Labor Day weekend at our cabin in the mountains. We look forward to seeing you soon.[5] Sincerely yours, [103]

6 To the Staff: In a recent meeting of all department heads, we decided that our firm must cut expenses if[1] we expect to make a reasonable profit for the year. We decided that one of the best ways to save during[2] the remainder of this fiscal year would be to travel less.

We should examine our plans carefully and take[3] only those trips that are absolutely necessary. Each of the department heads has agreed to make fewer[4] out-of-town trips to help meet our budget for this year.

Do you have any travel plans that you feel could be canceled[5] or postponed? Can you combine any of your trips?

Please let us know your revised travel schedule by the end of this[6] week. Ray Ford [122]

7 To the Staff: Beginning Monday, February 1, you will be eligible to join our monthly travel[1] investment program, a special program designed to help you save money for your annual vacation. The plan is[2] provided for the convenience of our employees; you are not required to participate, of course.

If you want[3] to participate in the plan, all you need do is fill out the attached membership application form, indicate[4] the amount you wish to save each month, and return the form to us in the enclosed envelope. We will deduct[5] the amount you indicate from your paycheck, place it in a special savings account for you, and pay you 7[6] percent interest.

You may withdraw the principal at any time. However, to receive the full 7 percent[7] interest, you must leave the money in the account for three full months. If you withdraw it before the end of the three months,[8] you will receive substantially less interest.

Start saving today; just let us know how much you wish to save each month.[9] When it is time for your vacation, you will have a ready cash reserve. William Blank [195]

8 Mr. Taylor: In today's mail I received a letter from Dr. Martin Smith, a professor of business at[1] Burlington State College. Dr. Smith will be teaching a graduate class this summer and would like to bring his students[2] to our airline office. He wants the class to learn as much as possible about the way a large airline uses[3] the computer in its everyday work.

Will you please make arrangements for Dr. Smith's class to visit our office[4] during the third week in July. There will be ten or fewer students in the class.

Thanks for your cooperation.[5] May Chan [101]

LESSON 59

Office-Style Dictation

1 *(As dictated)* Dear Mr. and Mrs. Hanson: We read in the newspaper recently that you will soon be celebrating your silver wedding anniversary. Perhaps you are wondering how to celebrate this wonderful event. We have a suggestion for you that we are sure you will like. (Indent the entire next paragraph.)

Treat yourselves to a vacation in Hawaii. This trip will certainly make your anniversary a memorable event. (The indention ends here.)

Many people have taken a trip to Hawaii to celebrate a special occasion. Don't you think you should do this too? Sincerely yours,

1 *(As it would be transcribed)* Dear Mr. and Mrs. Hanson: We read in the newspaper recently that you will soon be celebrating your[1] silver wedding anniversary. Perhaps you are wondering how to celebrate this wonderful event. We[2] have a suggestion for you that we are sure you will like.

Treat yourselves to a vacation in Hawaii. This trip[3] will certainly make your anniversary a memorable event.

Many people have taken a trip to[4] Hawaii to celebrate a special occasion. Don't you think you should do this too? Sincerely yours, [98]

3 Dear Sir or Madam: Will you please reserve a large room for me at the Hotel Washington in St. Louis, Missouri,[1] for June 2, 3, and 4. I will be in the city interviewing candidates for positions with my[2] company during that time, and I will need a room that has a sofa, a desk, and several chairs.

Because I will[3] be arriving late in the evening on June 2, I want to guarantee the reservation.

Please confirm this[4] reservation as soon as possible. Yours truly, [89]

4 Dear Mr. Pryor: More than a month ago we had the privilege of serving you as a guest at the Nashville[1] Motel. At the time you checked out, you left an unpaid balance of $138.50. Our[2] reservation clerk agreed to defer payment for two weeks until you returned to your home office.

Two weeks passed,[3] but we did not hear from you. Two more weeks passed, and we sent you a polite statement. Unfortunately, we still have[4] not heard from you.

We try to be accommodating and do everything we can to help our guests. Will you please[5] reciprocate by sending us your check today. This payment will help you to keep your good credit rating. Thanks for your[6] cooperation, Mr. Pryor. Very truly yours, [130]

5 Dear Ms. Martinez: We would like to invite you formally to join the State Travel Club, one of the largest[1] associations of its type in the world.

For only $20 a year you will be issued a[2] $25,000 travel accident insurance policy, you will receive our monthly travel magazine, and[3] you will be entitled to numerous travel services.

When you are a member of our organization,[4] we will help you make all your vacation plans. We will furnish you with marked maps that are easy to follow. We will[5] send you detailed maps of the cities you wish to visit. If you desire, we will make hotel, plane, and car rental[6] reservations for you.

In addition, we will send you our special identification card that will enable[7] you to cash checks up to $100 at any of our more than 1,000 offices located[8] throughout the continental United States.

You get all this for only $20. Doesn't it make sense to[9] join now, Ms. Martinez? Sincerely yours, [187]

6 Dear Mrs. Anderson: With the coming of spring, many of us are busy making plans to take trips abroad. One[1] should not overlook checking with the nearest office of the Department of Agriculture to find out in advance[2] what plants or foods are permitted entry into the United States. You should know the entrance status of common[3] plants and foods before you attempt to import them.

Each year people try to import items that could cause the[4] destruction of domestic plants because of pest infestation. The government inspectors keep watch at our ports of[5] entry to try to eliminate this risk.

It is the responsibility of the individual[6] traveler to be informed of what may be an environmental threat to our country. Please check with your nearest[7] government office before you attempt to bring anything into the United States. Very sincerely yours, [159]

7 Dear Dealer: On April 5, 1960, the first Silver Streak trailer was manufactured here at our plant in[1] Detroit, Michigan. That first model was made of lightweight metal and was designed for fuel economy.

We are[2] happy to say that this year's models are still made of lightweight metal and are still designed for fuel economy.[3] Each of the new models is totally self-contained. Each has its own living and sleeping quarters, and each has its[4] own kitchen and bath.

If you would like to know how easily you can become an authorized dealer and how profitable[5] our line of trailers can be for you, just write or call us. We will be looking forward to hearing from you.[6] Yours truly, [122]

8 Dear Ms. Jackson: The next time you need to travel by air to a business appointment in another city, don't[1] bother with the crowded parking lots at the airport. Leave your car at the Jennings Parking Lot, which is located[2] only three miles from the main entrance to the terminal. We will take you by air-conditioned bus to the terminal,[3] and we will pick you up when you call us after *you** return.

We are open 24 hours a day, and our[4] rates are much lower than those charged at the airport. Our lot is secure and well lighted. Your car will be safe with us.[5]

Park at our lot the next time you have occasion to *fly*† to another city. You will save time and money and[6] avoid frustration. Yours truly, [126]

Also correct:

*your

†go, travel

LESSON 60

3 Dear Friend: Here is an opportunity to join the International Travel Club at 50 percent of the[1] regular membership fee. We believe that you will agree this is an opportunity that you cannot afford[2] to let slip by.

When you are a member of the International Travel Club, you can effect savings of[3] up to 40 percent on your travel expenses. Our members are eligible for discounts on everything[4] from vacation clothing to hotel and motel accommodations.

International offers you the following[5] advantages:

1. Every month we will send you a travel newsletter filled with travel

tips, money-saving[6] advice, and information about new vacation resorts.

2. Our research department will recommend hotels,[7] airlines, and travel routes when you plan your next vacation.

3. One of our experienced counselors will help you[8] and your family obtain passports and visas.

If you are interested in becoming a member of the[9] International Travel Club, just sign and return the enclosed form along with your check for $10. You will be[10] making no mistake. Sincerely yours, [207]

4 Dear Mr. Jackson: As you will recall, I spoke with you on the telephone recently about the possibility[1] of my purchasing a lot at Lakeside Park, the retirement community that your organization[2] is developing near Mobile, Alabama. I will be retiring this summer, and I hope to build a[3] retirement home somewhere in the Mobile area.

Will you be in your office on Thursday, April 21, to[4] discuss my plans with me? I need answers to the following questions:

1. How large are the lots at Lakeside Park?

2.[5] Do the lots have trees?

3. What county is the development in?

Any help that you can give me will be greatly[6] appreciated. I am looking forward to hearing from you, Mr. Jackson. Sincerely yours, [137]

5 Dear Ms. Carver: We have just learned that you might be interested in applying for the position of tour director[1] with our travel agency. We know that you are experienced in planning, organizing, and conducting[2] tours and that you enjoy this interesting, challenging type of work.

The position that we have open is for someone[3] who is willing to travel, someone who is dedicated to the world of travel, and someone who is concerned[4] about the happiness of others. We know that you easily qualify for this position.

The starting[5] salary is $18,000, and we offer many fringe benefits to our employees.

If you are[6] interested in applying for the position of tour director with our organization, please fill out the[7] enclosed application form and return it to us. We hope to hear from you soon. Sincerely yours, [157]

6 Mr. Fleming: Several days ago I received a letter from Miss Mary White, one of our former employees.[1] Miss White worked for our travel agency about ten years ago and was regarded as one of our best people.[2] She left us to return to graduate school in the East.

Miss White would like to return to California, and[3] she wants to know if our company has any openings for part-time tour guides. She tells me that she would be able[4] to work two or three days each week but that she could not devote full time to the job.

Will you please consider hiring[5] Miss White on a part-time basis, Mr. Fleming. I think that she would be a definite asset to our[6] company. She is a knowledgeable, courteous, and efficient person. It would be in our self-interest to have[7] her back on our staff. Nancy Gomez [147]

7 Dear Mr. Lyons: Have you always wanted to take a vacation in the Far East but felt you could not afford[1] it? Now you can afford to make your dream come true. Our company, World Tours, has many tours from which you can choose for[2] much less money than you would ordinarily expect to pay.

Each tour includes deluxe hotel accommodations,[3] escorted sightseeing, and all meals. Taking one of our holiday tours is the carefree, economical[4] way to enjoy the vacation of a lifetime. You can visit the Far East for as little as $1,500[5] for two weeks.

Write us today for your free copy of our interesting booklet, *Touring the Far East.* Very[6] truly yours, [122]

CHAPTER 13

LESSON 61

3 Dear Mr. Parker: Many people begin physical fitness programs every day. Unfortunately, few people[1] continue with these programs. They find that exercising alone can be quite monotonous, and they quit after[2] only a few days' time.

If this has happened to you, Mr. Parker, I am sure you will be interested in[3] the special introductory offer now being made by the Los Angeles Health Club. During the month of[4] January you can join our club for a yearly membership fee of only $200, which is less than[5] half the regular fee.

In our well-equipped building at 206 Fourth Avenue, we have all the latest[6] exercise equipment. In addition, we have a swimming pool and a sauna. Our building is open from seven[7] in the morning until ten in the evening, and our experienced counselors are on duty at all times.

At[8] the Los Angeles Health Club you will find maintaining good physical health fun and easy. Don't delay; join today.[9] Just return the enclosed application along with your check. Sincerely yours, [194]

4 Dear Mrs. Adams: Before you leave on your vacation this summer, take a good look at your old camera. Can[1] it do everything you want it to do? Does it produce beautiful pictures every time? Are the colors bright and[2] clear? Is the picture in perfect focus?

If you cannot answer yes to these questions, you probably need to replace[3] your old camera. We recommend that you consider purchasing an Owens camera, one of the best[4] cameras on the market today.

When you have an Owens camera, you do not have to worry about[5] focusing the camera before you take a picture. You do not have to be concerned about having the proper[6] light. You can quit making these critical decisions yourself and let the Owens camera make them for you.

Don't[7] take a chance with your old camera on your vacation this year. Stop by your local photography shop and ask[8] to see the new Owens camera; you will be glad you did. Sincerely yours, [174]

5 Dear Friend: Would you like to see six new movies each month for one low fee? That is just what you can do when you subscribe[1] to our television service. The Home Television Theater brings into your home six of the best new movies[2] each month for the low price of only $12. Now you and your family can watch each of these movies in the[3] peace and quiet of your own living room.

We provide each of our customers with a listing for the entire month.[4] Each movie is shown several times during the month; therefore, you can choose the time that is most convenient for[5] you. Each movie is shown without commercial interruption, of course.

In order to take advantage of this service,[6] all you need do is call 555-6109. One of our people will come to your home and attach a[7] special device to your television set. Then each time you want to see one of the movies we are broadcasting,[8] all you need do is turn on your television set.

Take advantage of this great entertainment bargain; call us[9] today. Sincerely yours, [184]

6 Dear Miss Bates: Are you interested in the design and architecture of old houses? If you are, you are one of[1] thousands of people in the Chicago area who have become interested in this intriguing subject during[2] the past few years.

It is just for these people that we now publish *Homes of Yesterday,* a new quarterly[3] magazine devoted entirely to articles on the design, structure, and decor of old houses. You will not[4] find our magazine on the newsstands; it is sold through subscription only.

If you would like to receive a copy[5] of our latest issue, just write to our circulation department at 891 Tenth Avenue here in[6] Chicago. We will be glad to send you a copy free of charge. We are quite sure that when you have had an opportunity[7] to see this interesting new magazine, you will want to become a regular subscriber. Sincerely[8] yours, [161]

7 Dear Mr. Price: Do you enjoy the quiet, elegant atmosphere of a fine hotel? Do you expect the finest[1] accommodations and the best service when you travel? If you do, then you should stay at the Regency[2] whenever you visit Boston.

The Regency is one of the truly elegant hotels in the world. On the East[3] Coast it is in a class by itself. We have only 100 rooms, and they are ordinarily filled. This is[4] because travelers know that they can always depend on the Regency for first-class treatment.

The next time business[5] or pleasure brings you to Boston, stay at the Regency. There is no other hotel quite like it. Sincerely yours,[6] [120]

8 Dear Miss Teller: This is to acknowledge your letter to Mr. Sam Anderson requesting a business reference[1] for Mr. Martin Barns. Mr. Anderson is away from the city on an extended business trip and[2] will be unable to respond personally.

Therefore, your letter has been referred to me.

In my position[3] as assistant personnel director, I worked with Mr. Barns on many occasions. I always found him to[4] be a quiet, efficient person who completed every job quite conscientiously. He worked as social[5] director here at the hotel for a period of almost two years. Unfortunately, he was forced to quit his[6] job here because of health reasons. He developed asthma and moved to Phoenix, Arizona, six months ago.

I[7] am happy to recommend Mr. Barns for a position with your hotel. If you hire him, you will be making[8] no mistake. Sincerely yours, [165]

LESSON 62

3 Gentlemen: My family and I will be taking our annual vacation in June this year. We plan to drive[1] our trailer along the Gulf Coast through the states of Louisiana, Alabama, and Florida.

My teenage[2] son and daughter are both avid golfers. Therefore, we hope to stay in areas where they will be able to play[3] golf daily. In addition, we want to visit the major amusement parks in the vicinity.

Will you please[4] recommend trailer parks along our route that are close to the type of recreational facilities we want[5] to visit. We will appreciate any assistance that you will give us. A stamped, self-addressed envelope is[6] enclosed for your convenience in responding. Sincerely yours, [131]

4 Ladies and Gentlemen: I am quite interested in art, and I am planning a trip to Chicago in July[1] to visit the many excellent art galleries and museums there.

Although I like all types of art, I am[2] basically interested in seeing the National Museum of Modern Art, which was opened to the public[3] just last year. Will you please answer the following questions for me:

1. Is the museum open every day of[4] the year?
2. Is there a fixed admission charge?
3. Does the museum have a collection of motion pictures?

Any[5] information you can give me about the museum will be appreciated. Sincerely yours, [118]

5 To the Staff: As you know, there has been a great shortage of hotel rooms in the Los Angeles area during[1] the past three or four months. We have had difficulty in finding suitable accommodations for our out-of-town[2] business guests.

In order to alleviate the problem, we have decided to lease ten rooms at the Wellington[3] Hotel, which is located at 19206 Valley Road. This fine hotel is only a short drive from[4] our office building.

If you need accommodations for business guests from out of town, please contact Ms. Marsha Green[5] of our travel department; she will be able to tell you immediately if rooms are available for[6] the date you need them.

The basic rate of $65 per day will be charged to your department for each room[7] that you reserve. Max

Golden [145]

6 Dear Ms. Gordon: A delightful vacation awaits you at Rocky Mountain Resort.

On the shores of the Red River,[1] you will enjoy the beauty of gently rolling hills and the challenge of our 18-hole championship golf[2] course. In addition, you can play tennis or go fishing or swimming. You are sure to be impressed by our excellent[3] service and our beautiful, spacious rooms.

Let us make reservations for you at our magnificent resort.[4] Just call our toll-free number, (800) 555-8016. Very sincerely yours, [97]

7 To the Staff: Several months ago we placed a suggestion box in the main dining area of our office[1] building. We are happy to say that we have received hundreds of very good suggestions on how to make our[2] company more productive and a better place in which to work.

A number of you suggested that we convert our[3] present auditorium into a gymnasium for the exclusive use of our employees. We seriously[4] considered this suggestion for several weeks. While we make limited use of the auditorium[5] at the present time, we finally decided that it would be unwise to go to the expense that would be[6] necessary to convert it into a gymnasium.

Because we are definitely concerned with the health of[7] each of our employees, however, we have made arrangements with the Jefferson Health Club, which is located at[8] 80 24th Street, for group membership for our employees. If you wish to use the facilities of the[9] Jefferson Health Club, all that is necessary for you to do is stop by the personnel office and pick up[10] an identification card. Nancy Gray

[208]

LESSON 63

3 Dear Mr. King: If you are interested in an unusual vacation, we suggest that you take one of our[1] special tours to the great capitals of Europe this summer. For the low fee of $2,000, we will fly[2] you to London, Paris, and Rome.

You will spend a full week visiting London, a fascinating metropolis.[3] You will then fly to Paris, one of the most beautiful of the world's great cities. After a week there, you will[4] continue your vacation in Rome, one of the most interesting, intriguing cities of Europe. You will complete your[5] vacation by flying home in less than six hours on one of our supersonic jetliners.

You will stay in first-class[6] hotels in each city, and all meals and transportation fares are included. In addition, there will be special[7] sight-seeing tours of the historic sites in each city.

Don't delay; make your plans now for a once-in-a-lifetime[8] vacation. Call your travel agent for more details. Sincerely yours, [173]

4 Dear Mr. Stein: Here is an unusual idea for your vacation this summer. Rent a houseboat from our[1] company. Enclosed is a circular describing our modern, luxurious houseboats. We think you will find it quite[2] interesting.

You can be the captain of your own boat as you travel the more than 1,000 miles of rivers in[3] northern California. As you will see from the circular, you can visit the many marinas, restaurants,[4] and recreational facilities along the rivers. If you do not wish to travel the full 1,000[5] miles, you will still have the opportunity to fish, swim, and sightsee. If you prefer, you can just relax and enjoy[6] the many conveniences of your houseboat. The time is yours; you can spend it as you see fit.

Just read the[7] circular for more details. If you have any questions, we will be more than happy to answer them.

Be the captain[8] of your own boat this summer. Rent a houseboat from our company. Sincerely yours, [174]

5 Dear Friend: One of the best leisure activities is reading. Reading can stimulate your thinking, increase your knowledge,[1] and provide excellent entertainment.

The National Book Club offers you a wonderful opportunity[2] to purchase the latest books from all major publishers at prices that are well below those charged in local[3] bookstores. You may choose from a wide variety of books on every topic from current music to ancient[4] history.

Your initial membership brings you five books of your choice for only $1. If you are not completely[5] satisfied with your selections, you may return the books to us, and your membership will be canceled. To keep[6] your membership active, all you need do is purchase five books per year at our low discount prices.

Each month you will[7] receive a circular describing the books that are available. You select any of the books you want to[8] add to your library, and we will send them to you within ten days. You may purchase all the books, or you may decide[9] that you do not want any of the books in a particular month.

Don't delay; join the National Book Club[10] today. Select the five books you want from the enclosed list, and send your order along with $1 to us now.[11] You will receive your books shortly. Sincerely yours, [229]

6 Dear Mr. Cooper: If you would like to have a memorable, relaxing vacation without traveling thousands[1] of miles and without straining your budget, we suggest that you spend your next vacation at Clear Lake.

As you know,[2] Clear Lake is the largest, most beautiful lake in the state. You may not know, however, that many new recreational[3] facilities have been built in the past few years and that Clear Lake is now a nationally known resort[4] center. At Clear Lake you will find fishing, swimming, and boating facilities that are unsurpassed on the West Coast.[5] In addition, there are new hotels, motels, and restaurants located within a few blocks of the lake. There are[6] new, modern cabins located on the south side of the lake.

If you would like to have more

information about[7] Clear Lake, just write for our new circular. We will be glad to send it to you free of charge. Sincerely yours, [158]

7 Dear Mr. Gates: Several days ago I read in our local newspaper, *The Daily Star,* that the General[1] Amusement Corporation is planning to build a recreational park just east of the city near Ford Road.[2] This news disturbs me greatly because I live in the vicinity.

This neighborhood has already experienced[3] a large increase in the number of commercial establishments in the past few years. What was once a quiet[4] residential section of town is rapidly becoming a busy commercial district.

The traffic congestion[5] is particularly bad during the rush hours from 7 to 9 a.m. and 4 to 6 p.m. The[6] addition of a recreational park in the area would add to the problems that we now have.

I hope, Mr.[7] Gates, that you will use your influence as a member of the City Council to oppose this development.[8] Will you please let me know your feelings about this matter. Sincerely yours, [173]

LESSON 64

Office-Style Dictation

1 *(As dictated)* Dear Mr. Browne (that's spelled *B-r-o-w-n-e*): Many people take leisurely drives through the mountains on Sunday afternoons. If you are a Sunday driver (comma) there are several important things you should do when you drive on mountain roads. (Paragraph.) Be sure to keep your car on the right side of the road (semicolon) do not cross the center line. When you are driving downhill (comma) do not ride the brakes (that's *b-r-a-k-e-s*). Instead (comma) use a low gear. You should also be sure to drive at the posted speed limits. Remember that water boils faster at high altitudes. Therefore (comma) you should be sure to keep the radiator full of water at all times. (Paragraph.) Enjoy your Sunday trips by driving safely. Sincerely yours,

1 *(As it would be transcribed)* Dear Mr. Browne: Many people take leisurely drives through the mountains on Sunday afternoons. If you are a Sunday[1] driver, there are several important things you should do when you drive on mountain roads.

Be sure to keep your car[2] on the right side of the road; do not cross the center line. When you are driving downhill, do not ride the brakes. Instead,[3] use a low gear. You should also be sure to drive at the posted speed limits. Remember that water boils faster[4] at high altitudes. Therefore, you should be sure to keep the radiator full of water at all times.

Enjoy your[5] Sunday trips by driving safely. Sincerely yours, [109]

3 To the Staff: For the past two years we have been considering reducing our workweek from five days to four days. As[1] you know, we have asked you to give us your opinions and ideas on several occasions concerning this matter.[2]

The board of directors decided at its last regularly scheduled meeting on April 21 to[3] institute a trial four-day workweek in three departments beginning July 7. The advertising[4] department, the accounting department, and the personnel department will be open Monday through Thursday from eight[5] in the morning until six in the evening. These departments will be closed all day on Friday, Saturday, and Sunday.[6] All other departments will remain open Monday through Friday from nine in the morning until five in the[7] afternoon.

At the end of a six-month trial period, we will assess the results of the experiment.[8] We will then decide whether we should reinstate the five-day workweek in the three departments or change all departments[9] to a four-day week. James Burlington [187]

4 Dear Mr. Jackson: Now is the time for you and your family to begin participation in one of the[1] greatest sports activities in America, tennis. Tennis is a game for all ages; it helps you improve[2] your health, your strength, and your coordination. It also helps you acquire a high degree of concentration,[3] observation, and determination.

If you have wanted to join a tennis club but felt you could not afford to[4] do so, now is your chance to join our new club. As a charter member of the River Tennis Club, you will save[5] $100 on your first year's membership fee. You won't find a better club, and there will never be a better time[6] to join.

Save money and stay healthy; join the River Tennis Club today. Return the enclosed card in the[7] self-addressed envelope that is also enclosed. Yours truly, [150]

5 Dear Mrs. Martin: Would you like to have a beautiful swimming pool built in your yard for less than $3,000?[1] It may sound impossible, but the Davis Company can install a full-sized pool at your residence for[2] $3,000 or less.

Until a few years ago, most pools were constructed of concrete. They were quite expensive[3] to install and maintain. They had to be painted frequently and often cracked during the long, cold winter months.[4] In the past it was impractical for the average family to have a private swimming pool.

Today,[5] however, the Davis Company can install a durable plastic pool at a price that is well within almost[6] anyone's budget. Our low price includes the pool, its installation, and a beautiful set of poolside furniture.[7]

Davis swimming pools do not have to be painted and require very little special attention. They do not[8] develop leaks with normal use, and they do not crack in cold weather.

If you would like to have more information[9] about our pools, just fill out and return the enclosed card. You will be under no obligation, of course. Sincerely[10] yours, [201]

6 Dear Mr. Taylor: If you are like most people who live in city apartments, you do not have enough storage[1] space. Your closets are probably stacked to the ceiling with items that you need only occasionally.

It seems[2] there are never enough storage facilities for all the things you need to keep but seldom use. Apartment dwellers[3] ordinarily do not have a good place to keep such things as snow tires during the summer months. They usually[4] do not have a good place to keep Christmas decorations, tennis rackets, or other seasonal items.[5]

If you have this problem, our organization can be of assistance to you. The Eastern Storage Company,[6] which is located at 9206 Fourth Avenue, will rent you a private storage locker for only[7] $100 a year. Each locker is completely safe and weatherproof. It is 10 feet square, and there is room[8] to keep all the things you need only once or twice during the year. When you rent a locker from the Eastern Storage[9] Company, its contents may be insured for any value you place on them.

Take this opportunity, Mr.[10] Taylor, to clear your closets of items that you do not need on a daily basis. Rent one of our large, convenient[11] storage lockers; you will be glad you did. Sincerely yours, [231]

7 Dear Friend: We are happy to announce the grand opening of the Green Acres Miniature Golf Course located[1] at 610 College Street here in Mobile, Alabama.

At Green Acres we have the finest, most beautiful[2] miniature golf course in the South. Our course has 18 holes and contains both water and sand traps. Even the most[3] experienced player will find that Green Acres offers a real challenge.

From April 1 to April 15, we are[4] *offering** a 50 percent discount on the price of admission. Instead of paying our *regular*† fee of[5] $1 for each round of golf, you will pay only 50 cents.

Spend a leisurely hour or two at the Green Acres[6] Miniature Golf Course. We are open from 1 to 10 p.m. Sincerely yours, [135]

Also correct:
*giving, allowing
†usual, standard

LESSON 65

3 Dear Friend: If you are interested in taking an unusual vacation this summer, we have a suggestion[1] for you. Come to Denmark. In this country you will find a quaint combination of the old and the new.

You can visit[2] modern, up-to-date cities, or you can take a leisurely bicycle ride through the country. You can stay at[3] first-class city hotels, or you can stay at picturesque country inns.

If you enjoy music, sports, and the theater,[4] you will find them all in Denmark. If you enjoy the quiet, rural countryside, you will find that in Denmark too.

Come[5] to Denmark this summer; you will have a vacation that you will never forget. Sincerely yours, [117]

4 Dear Ms. West: Your employment agency has been referred to me by one of your clients, Miss Mary

Cunningham.[1] Miss Cunningham tells me that you have found a number of very good employees for her company.

At the present[2] time my travel agency is looking for a person to conduct guided tours to Mexico, Panama,[3] and Colombia. We need someone who can plan all aspects of international travel and who is accustomed[4] to handling a great deal of detailed work. We need a person who works well with people, and, of course, we need someone[5] who is bilingual. We will pay a beginning salary of $20,000 if we can find the[6] right person for the position.

If you have anyone on your lists who has all the qualifications for this[7] job, please let us know as soon as possible. We will be looking forward to hearing from you. Sincerely yours, [159]

5 Dear Mr. Young: Here is a success story that is hard to match. *The National Travel Magazine* began[1] publication only three years ago. During its first year as a bimonthly publication, the magazine had[2] a circulation of 500,000 copies and the gross revenue was less than $700,000.[3]

In its second year of publication, *The National Travel Magazine* became a weekly publication,[4] and its circulation reached 1 million. The gross revenue was more than $2 million. Last year the[5] circulation was nearly 3 million, and the gross revenue was almost $3 million.

To what can we[6] attribute this phenomenal record? Quite frankly, we believe it is good management and progressive marketing[7] techniques.

If you would like to advertise your sporting goods in a magazine that reaches 3 million people,[8] just fill out and return the enclosed self-addressed card. One of our representatives will be glad to come to your[9] office at your convenience to discuss a complete advertising program with you. Sincerely yours,

[198]

6 Dear Miss Lee: The Jenkins Sporting Goods Company is happy to announce the opening of our new store at[1] 1611 South Fourth Avenue here in Birmingham, Alabama.

At our new store, which is conveniently[2] located just across the street from the Southern Shopping Mall, you will find everything you will ever need in sporting[3] goods and sporting equipment. We have everything from bicycles to bowling balls. We have a complete line of[4] tennis rackets and tennis balls. We have golf clubs and shoes. We even carry a complete line of high-quality[5] binoculars.

Stop by our new location anytime during the first week, and you will receive a free gift just for[6] coming in. We will be open from 10 a.m. until 9 p.m. Monday through Saturday. We will be closed all[7] day Sunday. Sincerely yours, [145]

7 To the Staff: As you know, several months ago we initiated a new program here at Northern Airlines.[1] We asked each of you to make any suggestions that you felt would help our organization to increase its[2] efficiency and productivity.

Three or four of you felt that we needed a better means of internal[3] communications and suggested that we publish a company newspaper. The board of directors discussed this[4] recommendation at its last regularly scheduled meeting and decided that such a project was definitely[5] worthwhile. Therefore, we will issue a bimonthly newspaper to our company employees beginning in August.[6] The newspaper will contain articles and announcements concerning the company in general and our[7] employees in particular.

If you have any items that you consider worthy of publication, please[8] send them to Mr. Robert Cummings, who will be in charge of the newspaper during its first year of publication.[9] Alice Adams [184]

8 To the Staff: For the past year we have been publishing a company newspaper on a bimonthly basis. We[1] are pleased to say that the newspaper has served a real need in our organization. It has given management[2] a good place to make general announcements that affect all employees. It has also given every employee[3] a place to speak out on various issues affecting the company.

The only complaint we have had is[4] that the news is sometimes quite old before it is printed. Therefore, we have decided to change the publication[5] from bimonthly to weekly. The newspaper will be somewhat shorter, of course, but the news that it contains will be[6] much more up to date.

The first issue of the new weekly company newspaper will be published on Monday,[7] September 6. We hope you will give us your comments about it. Alice Adams [154]

CHAPTER 14

LESSON 66

3 Ladies and Gentlemen: On October 12, 13, and 14 we will have approximately 400 business[1] teachers from the six western states attending our twentieth annual fall conference. The conference will[2] be held in the Western Hills Conference Center, which is located at 210 Park Drive here in Portland, Oregon.[3]

We will be emphasizing reprographics at this year's conference. Because your company manufactures[4] several types of copiers and duplicators, we hope you will plan to have an exhibit at the conference.[5]

Each booth will contain 200 square feet of space and will be equipped with one large table. There will be an[6] adequate number of electrical outlets available at each booth, of course. A single booth will rent for[7] $100 for the three-day conference. The exhibit area will be open from 9 a.m. until[8] 6 p.m. every day.

If you are interested in renting a booth and exhibiting your equipment, please fill[9] out and return the enclosed application form today. We will be looking forward to hearing from you. Sincerely[10] yours, [201]

4 Dear Miss Peters: Last year we conducted a study of the office equipment in a well-known company in[1] the South. Some of the things we discovered might be of interest to you.

We found that the average age of the[2] typewriters in the company was 11 years. The average age of the calculators and adding machines[3] was 13 years. The average age of the duplicating machines was more than 15 years.

While many other[4] companies were taking advantage of the great advancements in modern technology, this particular[5] company was using old, out-of-date office equipment. The upshot was that the members of the staff were not working[6] as efficiently and effectively as they should have been.

Is your company in this predicament, Miss[7] Peters? If your typewriters, calculators, and other office machines are very old, your office staff may be[8] spending too much time and energy operating them. Your old machines could be costing you much more to operate[9] than it would cost to replace them.

The National Office Machines Company will be glad to send a[10] representative to analyze your office machines and discuss with you the low cost of replacing any of them[11] that are out of date. Just call or write us today. Very sincerely yours, [233]

5 Dear Mr. Masters: Do you have employees working in your company who could advance if they knew how to type?[1] Most large companies have a number of employees who cannot get ahead because they lack this particular[2] skill.

The Interstate Business College has an innovative typing course that can teach your employees to type in[3] a matter of only a few months' time. The self-teaching course is very well organized, and even elementary[4] school students who are only ten or eleven years of age have been able to learn to type easily[5] and quickly. What is more, your employees can learn to type right in your own office building; they will not have to take[6] the time and effort to attend a special class at a school or college.

Don't you think you should provide this course for[7] your employees, Mr. Masters? You can do them and yourself a favor by calling us today. Our telephone[8] number is 555-1106. Very cordially yours,[172]

6 Dear Educator: On Monday, September 23, the National Business Machines Manufacturing[1] Company will celebrate its 125th anniversary.

When we began manufacturing machines[2] back in the last century, we did not make any of the modern electronic instruments that we sell[3] today. We actually started our company by manufacturing typesetting equipment. We opened our[4] company in a converted warehouse on the outskirts of Flint, Michigan, and we are happy to say that our[5] modern manufacturing plant is located only a few short blocks away from the original site.

To[6] celebrate this significant anniversary, we are inviting the colleges and high schools in the Flint[7] area to bring their business students to visit our facilities. If your students are interested in modern[8] business technology, we extend to them a very special invitation to come to see our plant any[9] weekday during the month of September.

To make a reservation, all you need do is write for one. We hope[10] to hear from you soon. Sincerely yours, [207]

LESSON 67

3 Ladies and Gentlemen: In a recent issue of *Business World* I read about the business telephone system[1] that your company manufactures. My company, Bennington and Associates, conducts a major portion[2] of its business by telephone, and we are always looking for ways to decrease our expenditures.

We have four[3] offices in cities throughout the South–Houston, Dallas, Atlanta, and Miami. These offices are in contact[4] with each other 5, 10, or even 20 times each day. In addition, an executive in one city[5] often must speak with a client in a city served by one of our other offices.

Does your company have[6] a service whereby our four offices can communicate with each other during regular business hours for[7] a fixed fee? Is your system compatible with existing telephone equipment? Can you help us decrease our[8] overall telephone costs?

If you can help us, please ask one of your representatives to get in touch with us[9] as soon as possible. Very sincerely yours, [189]

4 Dear Depositor: We are happy to announce an innovative service here at the Greenville National Bank[1]—a cash machine.

Yes, our electronic cash machine, which is located near the main entrance to our bank on Park[2] Drive, can actually give you cash automatically. No longer will you have to wait in line in order to cash[3] a check. What is more, you can get cash at any hour of the day or night. Our cash machine is always open.

Because[4] you are already a depositor, all you need do to take advantage of this convenient new banking[5] service is stop by the bank between nine and three Monday through Friday and pick up your specially coded card.[6] Whenever you need cash, all you need do is insert your card into our cash machine and type your identification[7] number on the keyboard. You will receive any amount of cash up to a limit of $200[8] almost instantaneously.

We know you will enjoy this convenient new banking service here at the Greenville[9] National Bank. Sincerely yours, [186]

5 Mrs. Carson: As you will remember, last week the board of directors authorized us to invite representatives[1] from a number of office machines companies to come to our offices to demonstrate their new lines[2] of electric typewriters to our staff on April 21—or was it April 22?

At the time we[3] thought that we

would be replacing all the typewriters in our offices this year. Unfortunately, our budget[4] committee feels that it would not be wise for us to make such a large expenditure at this time. Therefore, we are[5] changing our plans. We are replacing half of the machines this year and half next year.

Will you please contact all department[6] heads to apprise them of this decision. Mark Porter [130]

6 Dear Ms. White: Did you know that you can have a second or third telephone in your home for less than 25 cents[1] a day? It is economical to have convenient extensions in every room of your home—or at least near[2] every room of your home.

Extension telephones actually add to the beauty and charm of your home. In the past,[3] telephones came in only one or two colors. Today, however, you can have extension telephones in a[4] wide variety of decorator colors. You can even move your telephones from one room of your house to[5] another if you wish to do so.

Yes, telephones have changed a great deal in the past few years. However, one thing[6] has not changed—quality. You can always depend on efficient, prompt service whenever you pick up your telephone.[7]

If you would like to have more information about extension phones for your home, please return the self-addressed[8] card. We will ask one of our representatives to call you at your convenience. Sincerely yours, [177]

7 To All Department Heads: On Saturday, April 14, we will be installing on-line computer terminals[1] in each office throughout our bank.

Each executive will have a great deal of information available in[2] a few seconds' time—checking account balances, savings account balances, and interest earned or owed on accounts.[3] All you need do is insert the customer's personal identification card into the computer[4] terminal and press a special code on the keyboard. You will have the needed information almost immediately.[5]

We will be conducting a series of training sessions during the entire week prior to the installation[6] of the terminals. Please plan to attend one of the sessions yourself. In addition, please bring any members[7] of your department who should learn to operate the terminals. Joseph Morgan [154]

LESSON 68

3 Mr. Gomez: As you know, six months ago we leased a small computer from the National Business Machines[1] Company in Cincinnati, Ohio. We wanted to try out the machine in our office to see if we could[2] reduce the amount of time it takes us to process orders, prepare financial statements, and to do other routine[3] office work.

Between you and me, I think the experiment is a failure. There is great reluctance on the[4] part of our office staff to use the computer. No major functions have been transferred to the machine in the six[5] months that we have been using it.

Our contract with the National Business Machines Company states that we can return[6] the computer with two months' notice. I am sure that you understand the situation better than I. Under[7] the circumstances, however, I suggest that we return the computer at the end of March.

Will you please[8] let me know your feelings about this matter as soon as possible. Jane Winters [174]

4 Dear Mr. Trent: Do your office employees spend hundreds of hours every month posting customers' purchases to[1] their accounts? Do your employees spend an inordinate amount of time checking and reviewing account totals?[2] Do your employees need several days to prepare end-of-month reports?

If you are experiencing those kinds[3] of problems, your company is no different from thousands of others. However, we think we have the solution[4] to your troubles. Install a General computer. When you have a General computer, the routine office[5] tasks that formerly took hours, days, or even weeks can be done in a matter of only a few minutes' time.[6] Your office employees will be free to do other, more challenging–and productive–work. In addition, it will[7] actually cost you less money in the long run.

Are you interested? If you are, just contact the General[8] Computer Company; our telephone number is 555-8806. If you wish, you may write to us at[9] 8641 East 27 Street. Let us help you take the drudgery out of your office work and[10] reduce expenses at the same time. Sincerely yours, [210]

5 Dear Miss Marsh: Has your bank ever leased an expensive computer only to find that you were not actually getting[1] your money's worth? Have you ever bought a small computer only to find out later that it was not capable[2] of performing the required work in your bank?

Only a few years ago those kinds of problems were prevalent[3] throughout the banking industry. Today, however, you can purchase or lease a computer that is especially[4] designed for your use–and for your use only. You do not have to pay for features that you do not need. In[5] addition, the computer will perform every function that is necessary in your particular business.

What[6] is more, you will pay only a minimal amount if you purchase or lease a computer from the General[7] Computer Company. For more information, just write to us at the address shown on the letterhead. Sincerely[8] yours, [161]

6 Dear Mr. McGuire: Is your inventory control system modern and up to date? If you are operating[1] your business today with yesterday's technology, you are probably losing money. You could even be losing[2] customers to your competitors.

If you are having those kinds of problems, we have a suggestion for you.[3] Let us bring your inventory control system up to date. For a fee that is much less than you might imagine,[4] we can install an inventory control system for you that will speed up your operations significantly.[5] In addition, it can help you decrease the number of errors made in filling orders.

Through the use of[6] high-speed computers, each of your employees can determine the exact status of every item you sell.[7] In less than a minute any employee can determine whether or not an item is in stock, what the current[8] price is, and how long it will take for delivery. No longer will your salespeople give misquotations to[9] customers. Each employee will have up-to-date, accurate information available on a moment's notice.[10]

If you want more information about our inventory control system, just call us at (800)[11] 555-6106. You will be making no mistake by calling us, Mr. McGuire. Sincerely yours, [238]

7 Dear Mrs. Michaels: For the past few years you have attended the annual office machines exhibit in[1] Chicago, where we have shown our new products. This year's exhibit will be held at the Scott Hotel during the week of[2] September 17. The Scott Hotel is located on the corner of Main Street and Park Drive.

We cordially[3] invite you to visit our booth and see the many fascinating new machines that we will be displaying. Our[4] new office machines are quite different from those we have exhibited in the past. We think you will be[5] particularly interested in the small, economical computers that we will be showing for the first time this[6] year.

We look forward to seeing you in Chicago and to speaking with you about our new products. Sincerely[7] yours, [141]

LESSON 69

Office-Style Dictation

1 *(As dictated)* Dear Mr. Kennedy: We have received the digital watch that you sent to us for repair. When we received (make that *examined*) it thoroughly (comma) we discovered that it had been dropped on a hard surface. That is why it did not operate properly. (Paragraph.) Our guarantee does not insure (no, make that *does not provide*) protection against damage to our products. Therefore (comma) we cannot replace the watch (make that *repair or replace the watch*) for you at no charge. (Paragraph.) If you would like us to repair it (comma) please send us your check for $50 (comma) which is the total cost of repairs and handling. When we receive your check (comma) we will repair your watch and return it to you. (Paragraph.) If you have any questions about our service (comma) please contact the dealer in Dallas from whom you purchased the watch. Sincerely yours, (Let's send a copy of this letter to Mr. Davis.)

1 *(As it would be transcribed)* Dear Mr. Kennedy: We have received the digital watch that you sent to us for repair. When we examined[1] it thoroughly, we discovered that it had been dropped on a hard surface. That is why it did not operate[2] properly.

Our guarantee does not provide protection against damage to our products. Therefore, we cannot repair[3] or replace the watch for you at no charge.

If you would like us to repair it, please send us your check for $50,[4] which is the total cost of repairs and handling. When we receive your check, we will repair your watch and return[5] it to you.

If you have any questions about our service, please contact the dealer in Dallas from whom you purchased[6] the watch. Sincerely yours, [125]

3 Dear Mr. Edwards: If you are looking for the perfect gift for a business associate, we have a suggestion[1] for you. Purchase a National AM-FM radio. A National radio is the perfect[2] addition to any business office. It can provide soft background music that is welcome almost anywhere.

Enclosed[3] is a circular that describes the new National models. We are sure that you will find one that will make a[4] perfect gift. You can choose from 15 models in a wide variety of styles and colors.

If you would like to[5] order one of our beautiful radios, just fill out the form that is attached to the enclosed circular and[6] return it to us. When we receive it, we will send your radio immediately. You need send no money;[7] we will bill you later. Sincerely yours, [147]

4 Dear Sir or Madam: Do you know that music can actually help you sell the products in your store? Yes, it is a[1] fact that the right kind of music contributes to an atmosphere that is conducive to increasing sales.

The[2] National Music Company can install a music system in your store that will provide just the right type of music[3] at the right time of day. We can provide spirited, sprightly music in the early morning and late afternoon[4] hours and slow, restful music at other times. If you wish, we can program the selections that you yourself[5] particularly enjoy.

If you would like to have one of our experienced representatives come to your store[6] to explain the great benefits of a National music system, just call or write us. Let us help you make your[7] store a nicer, more enjoyable place in which to shop and increase your sales at the same time. Sincerely yours, [159]

5 Dear Miss Cunningham: Are you physically tired at the end of the day? Do you have a backache when you go home in[1] the evening? The cause could be your chair. Most of us who work in offices spend at least 40 percent of our time[2] sitting at our desks. Few of us, however, think of the importance of the chair in which we sit.

Doctors have been[3] telling us for many years that we should pay more attention to the chairs we place in our offices. Many doctors[4] actually recommend that every employee have a posture chair.

We will be glad to send one of our[5] representatives to your office to show you our line of posture chairs. In fact, we will let you have two or three chairs[6] for a week's trial free of charge. We know that you and your staff will be more comfortable and less tired at the end[7] of the day when you have posture chairs.

Call or write to us today. You will be under no obligation, of course.[8] Sincerely yours, [163]

6 Ladies and Gentlemen: How badly would your business suffer if your records were suddenly destroyed by water[1] or fire? Most businesses would suffer greatly; some would not be able to survive.

Are your valuable records kept[2] in waterproof and fireproof cabinets? If they are not, you could be taking a great risk with your company's future.[3]

In the past few years many wise managers have switched from ordinary metal files to General files that[4] are waterproof and fireproof. General files come in several styles and sizes. You can order them to hold[5] standard-sized or legal-sized papers. You can order two-drawer, four-drawer, or five-drawer files.

Enclosed are a[6] circular and a price list describing all the files available through your local General dealer, the Troy Office[7] Supply Store located at 680 Market Street. Stop in soon and examine the durable, attractive[8] General files.

The Troy Office Supply Store is open Monday through Friday from 9 a.m. until 5 p.m. They will[9] be happy to show you our entire line of files. Sincerely yours, [192]

7 To the Staff: As you know, we are installing a new electronic cash register at every sales desk throughout[1] the store. If all goes well, we will complete the changeover to the new system on Thursday, March 24.

There are[2] several reasons for replacing our old cash registers. They are as follows:

1. It will take each cashier only[3] two or three seconds to register an *item.** By using the light pen that reads the special codes on the[4] containers, the cashier can work more quickly and more accurately.

2. Our inventory control system will be[5] significantly improved. Each item sold will be deducted from the master inventory list immediately.[6] We will know in a matter of a few seconds how many items have been sold and when we should reorder.[7]

3. We will eventually reduce our overhead expenses. Although it will take several years to[8] recover our initial investment, our *expenses*† will be substantially lower in the long run.

On Monday,[9] March 21, we will hold training sessions for everyone who will be operating the new cash registers.[10] The sessions will be held at 9 a.m., 2 p.m., and 4 p.m. Please plan to attend the session that is most[11] convenient for you. Tom Wade [225]

Also correct:
*purchase
†costs

LESSON 70

3 To the Executive Committee: As you know, Independence Day is on Thursday this year. The board of directors[1] of our company decided at its last meeting to close our office for the four-day period beginning[2] July 4.

Several weeks ago we scheduled an executive committee meeting for Friday, July[3] 5. Because our office will be closed on that date, it will be necessary for us to postpone the meeting until[4] the following week. We are tentatively rescheduling the meeting for Wednesday, July 10, at 9 a.m.[5] in the boardroom.

If this time and date are not satisfactory with you, please let me know immediately.[6] If I do not hear from you, I will assume that the time and date are convenient for you. Allen Case [138]

4 Mr. Simmons: There is confusion among the personnel in our organization about the date of our[1] next company holiday. As you know, we have celebrated Washington's Birthday on February 22[2] for many years. The last company bulletin makes no mention of February 22 as a[3] company holiday this year. The next holiday apparently is scheduled for February 18. Perhaps[4] a mistake was made when the company calendar was printed.

Many of our employees are postponing their[5] plans until a clarification is made. If the date has been changed, I think it would be judicious to issue[6] a memorandum explaining the reason. If the calendar is wrong, I suggest that a new one be printed as soon[7] as possible. Mike Edwards [145]

5 To the Staff: Yesterday Calvin James, our company controller, came to my office to discuss a problem that[1] has developed. He brought with him two postdated checks that a sales representative had accepted during the[2] past week. One was dated March 21, and one was dated March 22. This is more than three months in the future.[3]

It is a policy of our company not to accept postdated checks for payment of goods that are to[4] be delivered immediately. If customers wish to postpone payment, they may sign a promissory note.[5] The note will, of course, include an interest charge.

We must pay 14 percent interest on money that we borrow from[6] local banks. Therefore, you can easily understand why we cannot give our customers three months to pay their bills.[7] We would actually be financing their inventories for them. Cynthia Drake [154]

6 Dear Marvin: I want to take this opportunity to congratulate you on your company's twentieth[1] anniversary. This marks a real milestone in the progress of your organization.

I remember well the day[2] you opened your first small store in Birmingham. It doesn't seem possible that your organization could have become[3] one of the world's largest, best-known office machines manufacturers in so short a period of time.

I[4] had originally planned to come

to Alabama to congratulate you in person on this significant[5] anniversary. Unfortunately, I will not be able to do so. I will be out of the country[6] on a business trip for the next three weeks. Therefore, I must postpone my visit to the South until after the first[7] of the year. I hope you will let me take you to dinner as a belated anniversary celebration[8] in January. Sincerely yours, [167]

7 To the Staff: On Monday, August 6, our company will begin using a central postage meter. We will no[1] longer use regular postage stamps on correspondence to be mailed from our office.

We are instituting a[2] new procedure for the handling of our correspondence. A mail clerk will pick up the mail from each office twice a[3] day. The pickup will be at approximately ten in the morning and four in the afternoon. Please have all[4] correspondence ready and waiting at these times. The mail clerk will sort and weigh each piece of correspondence and register[5] the proper amount of postage on it.

If you have any questions about this procedure, please contact Ellen[6] James, head of the mail room. Bill Williams [127]

8 To All Department Heads: The United States Postal Service has asked American businesses to be sure that[1] ZIP Codes are included on each piece of correspondence that is mailed.

If ZIP Codes are not used in the addresses[2] of the correspondence that we mail, delivery will be delayed. If they are used, the mail can be sorted[3] mechanically and delivered rapidly.

Please be sure that every person in your department uses ZIP Codes on[4] all correspondence. If you do not have access to a directory, please let me know; I will be happy to[5] make one available to you. Arthur Strong [108]

CHAPTER 15

LESSON 71

3 Dear Miss Poland: Too seldom do the owners and managers of department stores take time to say to their preferred[1] customers, "Thanks for shopping with us." However, we want to take this opportunity to thank you for your[2] confidence in us and in our service. As a token of our gratitude, we are enclosing an invitation[3] to attend a special sale that will be open to our preferred customers only.

As you know, we have two 3-day[4] clearance sales annually. The first is held in January; the second is held in July. For the first[5] time this year, we are beginning our sale one day early—only for preferred customers. On Monday, January[6] 10, we are opening our doors at 10 a.m., which is our regular opening time. However, we will[7] close at 5 p.m. We will reopen our doors at 6 p.m.—but only to our preferred customers. From 6[8] p.m. until 10 p.m. you will be able to make great savings on everything from men's, women's, and children's[9] clothing to furniture and household furnishings. Many items will be discounted as much as 50 percent.[10]

In order to attend this special event, all you need do is present this letter at the Main Street entrance to[11] our store between 6 and 9:30 p.m. You will be admitted to the largest, best sale our store has ever[12] held. We will be looking forward to seeing you on Monday evening, January 10. Very sincerely yours,[13] [260]

4 Dear Mr. Bates: Several weeks ago my company, The Standard Sales Corporation, ordered 1,000 four-page[1] circulars from your advertising company. We had hoped to use the circulars to help introduce our[2] new line of sporting goods. We wanted to mail the circulars by the 10th of June in order to attract shoppers[3] before Independence Day.

Here it is June 15, and we have not yet received the circulars. If we do not[4] have them in our hands within the next three or four days, we will be forced to cancel our order.

Please let us know what[5] your company intends to do about this matter. Yours truly, [112]

5 Gentlemen: The bids for the construction of the new addition to our motel have been opened. We are sorry[1] to tell you that yours was not accepted. The contract will be awarded to the Edwards Corporation. Your bid[2] was the third lowest submitted to us.

As you know, we were quite impressed with the three 8-unit apartment buildings[3] you constructed on State Street. We know that without question you are capable of doing high-quality work.[4] Because of financial constraints, we are compelled to accept the lowest bid.

Thank you for the time and effort that[5] you and your staff invested in preparing your bid; we appreciate your cooperation. Sincerely yours,[6] [120]

6 To the Members of the Board: Because of the critical housing shortage in Springfield, we are having a very[1] difficult time finding suitable living accommodations for the executives that we want to transfer[2] from our regional offices throughout the United States to our company headquarters here in this city.[3] During the past year we have had difficulty in getting some of our better people to transfer here because[4] they felt that they would not be able to find houses for their families. On two or three occasions we have had[5] to rent hotel rooms for as long as three months for our executives because they could not locate adequate houses.[6]

I believe that it would be a good idea to lease at least three 2-bedroom apartments on a long-term basis[7] for the use of our people who transfer into the city. If we had good living accommodations[8] immediately available, I think it would be much easier for us to get our promising people to[9] accept positions here at our company headquarters.

Do you agree? Please let me know your feelings on this matter[10] as soon as possible. If the majority of the officers of our organization think this is[11] a good idea, I will lease at least three 2-bedroom apartments as soon as they are available. I believe[12] that we will pay less in the long run and that we will be able to get our best people to accept positions[13] here in Springfield. Janet Burns [265]

7 Miss Stone: Thank you very much for sending me a copy of the manuscript for the public relations brochure[1] that you plan to distribute to those who attend the twentieth anniversary convention of our[2] organization in Baltimore, Maryland, next April.

In general, I am very well pleased with the manuscript.[3] However, I think that printing 1,000 eight-page brochures will be quite expensive. I believe that we can get[4] the same impact from a four-page brochure.

I am enclosing the manuscript that you mailed to me with six paragraphs[5] marked in red pencil. If you delete these paragraphs, I am sure that you will be able to fit the rest of[6] the information in a four-page brochure.

Will you please let me know if you agree with me. Agnes Carter [139]

8 Miss Lexington: In the past few months I have had a large number of complaints from customers concerning the way[1] we handle telephone inquiries. It seems that it is very difficult for a potential customer to[2] get proper information about our goods and services by telephoning our company. It is essential[3] that we improve our telephone communications procedures.

Three weeks ago I asked a member of each[4] department in our company to serve on a special committee to establish a new procedure for handling[5] telephone inquiries. This committee has written what I believe is a very practical, sensible[6] guide for handling all telephone inquiries.

Mr. Larry Smith, who chaired the committee, is sending you 100[7] two-page charts that should be distributed to each person who answers telephone inquiries. Will you please see[8] that each person who needs a copy receives one in the next day or so. Harry Moore [175]

LESSON 72

3 Dear Dr. Miller: Congratulations on the publication of your new books on automotive mechanics[1] (both of them). It has been our pleasure to work with you on the revisions and to publish the texts for you.

You are[2] to be commended for having included so many innovative techniques in the texts. The materials[3] you include are quite relevant to the needs of today's students. It is my opinion, Dr. Miller, that your[4] two books are vastly superior to similar books on the market. We have received several very[5] complimentary letters from the reviewers of your manuscripts (see the enclosed summary).

Fourteen copies of[6] each book will be sent to you shortly. If you want additional copies, please let me know.

Thank you for doing such[7] a thorough, careful job and for meeting your deadlines. This helped us a great deal. We are looking forward to very[8] good sales of your two books and to working with you on other publications in the future. Sincerely yours, [179]

4 Dear Miss Wheeler: Congratulations on your recent graduation from Eastern Business College. We know that you[1] will benefit greatly from your college education and that you will make a significant contribution[2] to our society and to the business world.

We at the Webber Department Store are especially proud of[3] those of you who graduated in the top 10 percent of your class. To express our congratulations to you[4] in a very special way, we are sending you a gift certificate (see the attached envelope). You may use[5] the gift certificate for: (1) a radio, (2) a tape recorder, or (3) an electronic calculator.[6]

All you need do to receive your gift is present the certificate to one of our sales representatives[7] at our main store at 610 East 21 Street here in Miami. We will be looking forward to seeing you[8] in our store in the next week or so. Sincerely yours, [170]

5 Dear Mr. and Mrs. Washington: Enclosed are two complimentary tickets for the premiere of our first[1] theatrical production this season. Because you are dedicated supporters of the Wichita Community[2] Theater, we wanted you to have tickets for two of the best seats in the house.

We have appreciated your[3] support over the years, but we have rarely had the opportunity to tell you so. We hope these tickets will help[4] us in showing our gratitude to you.

Remember, all performances this year will be held in the Wichita[5] Theater (formerly the East Side Cinema). The theater is located at 216 Elm Drive.

We hope that you[6] will enjoy our first production of the season and that you will attend every one of the six remaining shows.[7] Very sincerely yours, [144]

6 Dear Ms. Garcia: Thank you very much for your letter congratulating me on my appointment as[1] superintendent of schools. The position of superintendent is a difficult, challenging one. With the help of[2] fine citizens like you, however, I will be able to do the job satisfactorily.

The school board has[3] established ten major objectives for the coming year. Most of the objectives deal specifically with the[4] critical problems of: (1) maintaining high-quality education during a period of declining[5] enrollment and (2) improving the tax base for support of the public schools.

When you have had an opportunity[6] to study the objectives, I hope you will let me have your suggestions for implementing them. Thanks, Ms. Garcia,[7] for your continued support. Sincerely yours, [149]

7 Dear Ms. Fenton: Thank you for your letter concerning the article I wrote in the Saturday, November[1] 21, issue of *Business Day.* The statistics that I quoted were based on a report published by the National[2] Opinion Survey Company, which is located in Springfield. However, the conclusions were my own, and[3] I take full responsibility for them.

I was trying to show in the article that public opinion[4] concerning mass transportation has changed significantly during the past few years. Although there is a great deal[5] of controversy about the best means of financing mass transit systems, many people believe that: (1) there[6] should be a public transportation system in every major city and (2) the use of private vehicles[7] in congested areas should be curtailed.

I am sorry that you do not agree with my opinions, Ms. Fenton.[8] However, I look forward to hearing from you concerning other articles that I will be writing for[9] future editions of *Business Day.* Sincerely yours, [190]

8 Mrs. Small: As you know, we will be celebrating a very special day on Tuesday, February 24[1]–our company's twentieth anniversary. We are planning: (1) a reception, (2) a banquet, and (3)[2] an open house.

I would like you to be in charge of all arrangements for the banquet, Mrs. Small. If you will accept[3] this major responsibility, you will have the gratitude of the executive committee.

Will you[4] please let me know your decision as soon as possible. Janice Cunningham [94]

LESSON 73

3 To the Staff: The Jennings Publishing Company is planning a reception in honor of Ms. Judy Gray, who[1] will be retiring after many years of service.

As you know, Ms. Gray is the author of the college text,[2] *Principles of Accounting.* Ms. Gray is a unique person who has always been willing to help others. Her willingness[3] to help and her cheerfulness have affected the attitudes of every one of us. She has been a true asset[4] to our company, and we will miss her greatly after her retirement.

The reception will be held at the[5] Valley Country Club, which is located at 2717 Route 21, on Saturday, August[6] 15, at 6 p.m. The reception will be followed by a formal dinner at 7 p.m.

If you plan[7] to attend, please fill out the top half of the enclosed card and return it to us along with your check for $15[8] (no cash please). Retain the bottom half; it will serve as your admission ticket. If you would like to contribute[9] toward a gift for Ms. Gray, please send any amount you wish along with the card. Janet Miller [197]

4 Dear Mr. Powers: Congratulations on the purchase of your new Lexington automobile. You have chosen[1] one of the finest, most beautiful cars on the market today.

The type of gasoline that you use in your car[2] will have a great effect on its performance, of course. It is very important that you use only lead-free[3] gasoline. Your new Lexington is equipped with a special converter that will be permanently damaged if you[4] use gasoline that contains even a small amount of lead. We recommend premium lead-free gasoline that[5] is available at most major service stations.

All new Lexington cars are finished with the very best paints[6] available today. Over the years, however, the finish will deteriorate if it is not protected[7] from the ravages of sun, wind, and rain. To retain the bright, beautiful finish, we recommend that you use[8] Lexington car wax, the wax that is especially formulated to protect the finish of our automobiles.[9]

When you purchased your car, you received a booklet that contains complete instructions on how to operate and[10] maintain your car. We hope you will read it carefully. After you have read it, we will be happy to answer any[11] questions you may have. Sincerely yours, [227]

5 Dear Ms. Pierce: We were very glad to see you when you came to the First National Bank last week. We want to congratulate[1] you on your decision to purchase three 2-year time certificates. By placing your ready cash in time[2] deposits you have assured yourself of the highest interest rate allowed by law, and your funds will be completely[3] safe.

As you know, the principal will draw 10 percent interest for two years. At the end of the two-year period,[4] you may redeem your certificates. If you want to retain your investment, however, we will reinvest the[5] principal plus the accumulated interest in a new time deposit at the prevailing interest rate.

We[6] know you are pleased with your decision to purchase time certificates at the First National Bank, Ms. Pierce. If we[7] can be of further service to you in any way, we hope you will let us know. Sincerely yours, [157]

6 Dear Mr. Stern: Three months ago you purchased a fully equipped Lexington van from our agency here in Mobile,[1] Alabama. Because you have not brought the van in for its three-month checkup, we are wondering what the problem[2] could be.

Perhaps you have not yet had an opportunity to take the van out of town in order to put[3] it to a real test. Perhaps it is running so well that you decided it was not necessary to bring it[4] in for maintenance. Perhaps it simply slipped your mind. Whatever the reason, we hope you will take this opportunity[5] to call us at 555-8616 to make an appointment for a checkup.

We are enclosing[6] a photographic copy of the factory warranty that you received when you purchased the van. To retain[7] the unconditional one-year guarantee, you must bring your vehicle in for routine maintenance. Please retain[8] the validity of your warranty; call us for an appointment now. Cordially yours, [176]

LESSON 74

Office-Style Dictation

1 *(As dictated)* Dear Mr. Lopez: The

name of the accountant who handles our business affairs is D. C. Brown (check the spelling on that name; it may be *B-r-o-w-n-e*). His office is located at 456 North Fifth Avenue, Chicago, Illinois 60607 (please verify the street address and the ZIP Code).

My partners and I had many meetings with Mr. Brown when we incorporated. All of us were impressed with him. His suggestions have proved to be worthwhile and have saved us a great deal of money.

I know you will find Mr. Brown to be just as efficient if you hire him to work for you. Sincerely yours,

1 *(As it would be transcribed)* Dear Mr. Lopez: The name of the accountant who handles our business affairs is D. C. Brown. His office is[1] located at 456 North Fifth Avenue, Chicago, Illinois 60607.

My partners[2] and I had many meetings with Mr. Brown when we incorporated. All of us were impressed with him. His[3] suggestions have proved to be worthwhile and have saved us a great deal of money.

I know you will find Mr. Brown to be[4] just as efficient if you hire him to work for you. Sincerely yours, [93]

3 Mr. Long: As you know, my staff and I have been traveling throughout the state encouraging potential students[1] to come to State College next fall. We have just returned from our journey, and we are pleased to report that this year's trip[2] was extremely successful. We should find an increase in enrollment next year due mainly to the success of this[3] tour.

This year we invited four State College students to travel with us. We selected four students who we felt[4] would be good ambassadors of our college and of our student body—James Smith, Betty Brown, Max Tate, and Janet[5] Garcia. During the sessions we found that the high school students developed rapport with the college students. They[6] were able to communicate very well.

Attached is a list of prospective students, their addresses, and the[7] names of their high schools. We already have definite commitments from more than 50 percent of these students. Bob[8] Davidson [162]

4 Dear Customer: Thank you for your patience with us while we remodeled our hardware store. We knew that we would be[1] inconveniencing you, but we also knew that our store was much too small to accommodate all the various lines[2] of goods we wanted to stock.

As you probably know, we purchased the empty building next door and have now doubled[3] the size of our store. Our plans are to double our inventory as well. You should be able to find almost any[4] hardware item that you need in our expanded store.

We are planning our grand opening on Saturday, April[5] 10, at 10 a.m. We hope you will plan to be with us then. The card that is enclosed will admit you to a[6] room of specially priced sale items. Cordially yours, [130]

5 Dear Member: After long hours of careful deliberation, the executive board of the Western Real Estate[1] Association has reached the difficult decision that dues must be raised for the coming year. This decision[2] was unanimous.

The members of the board realize that everyone is faced with an increase in the cost of living,[3] but they also realize that our organization cannot continue to deliver the same fine services[4] to its members without receiving extra funds. As you know, we have maintained a high level of service and[5] have initiated many new programs during the past few years.

The new dues approved by the board will be[6] $50 per year. As you will recall, your dues entitle you to our professional magazine, our yearbook,[7] and all special circulars and brochures relating to real estate law.

We are sure you will understand that it[8] is essential for us to increase our dues, and we hope you will continue your membership in our organization.[9] Incidentally, your dues are deductible expenses for income tax purposes. Sincerely yours, [199]

6 Dear Mrs. Cummings: Our accountant suggested that we examine our records and write to each customer who[1] has not used his or her charge account in the past few months. We examined our accounts, and we were very unhappy[2] to learn that you have not used your charge account with our store for more than a year.

We are wondering if we have[3] done something to offend you or if you have found something wrong with our service. We hope that we are not at fault, but[4] if we are, we sincerely apologize.

If you have simply not been to our store during the past year, we hope[5] you will pay us a visit soon. We are sure you will be pleased with the many excellent buys that are available[6] in every one of our departments. We hope to see you in our store soon. Sincerely yours, [137]

7 Mr. Edwards: Congratulations on the large sale you made to the Jefferson Supply Company. Never before[1] has that company placed such a large order with our firm. I am sure that your knowledge, skill, and personality[2] had a great deal to do with the sale. You are to be commended.

This large sale should provide you with a sizable[3] commission at the end of the fiscal year. Keep up the good work. Nancy White [74]

8 Dear Ms. James: Thank you for your letter of Friday, April 23. Please forgive me for not *answering** sooner;[1] I have been out of the city on an extended business trip. When I returned, I found your letter on my desk.[2]

It is a pleasure, Ms. James, to accept your invitation to speak at the graduation ceremonies of[3] Madison High School. I will *speak*† on the subject of careers available to youth today. I will touch on careers[4] that require high school diplomas, and I will also touch on careers that require a college degree.

I am[5] looking forward to being with you on June 2 at 8 p.m. at the Madison High School auditorium.[6] Sincerely yours, [123]

Also correct:
*responding
†talk

LESSON 75

3 Dear Mrs. Davis: You will recall that we sent you three statements for the purchases you made in January[1] and February. These statements were sent once a month for the past three months. To date, however, we have received neither[2] a check nor an acknowledgment from you.

Needless to say, we cannot afford to continue to send you statements[3] and receive no explanation or payment from you. This letter is being written as a friendly gesture[4] to remind you that you will have until June 30 to pay your bill in full. If we do not have your check by that[5] date, we will have no recourse but to turn the matter over to our attorneys.

Please do not force us to resort[6] to this course of action. We will appreciate your cooperation, Mrs. Davis. Yours truly, [138]

4 Dear Miss Simms: As you will remember, several weeks ago I came to your home furnishings store and ordered new[1] drapes for my living room, my dining room, and my den. I chose the same style and fabric for each of the rooms. The[2] material was light brown and quite soft and delicate.

Last week Miss Wilson, one of your decorators, came to my[3] home to take the measurements for the drapes. She stayed almost an hour and was quite thorough in checking to be sure that[4] every measurement was exact. Yesterday she returned to install the drapes. When she arrived, I was surprised with[5] the drapes that she brought. They were yellow instead of light brown; the material was coarse instead of soft and delicate.[6] The drapes were definitely not what I wanted for my home, and I could not accept them.

Miss Wilson showed me[7] a copy of the order with my signature. The fabric ordered was No. 608, which is the same number[8] as that shown on the drapes themselves. It seems that the wrong fabric number was entered on the order blank. You can[9] easily see that the problem is yours; it is not mine.

Under the circumstances, I must insist that the drapes[10] be remade or that you refund my money promptly. Yours truly, [212]

5 Dear Dr. Weston: We are currently making plans for our annual fall business conference in Albany.[1] The conference will be held October 11, 12, and 13 in the Albany Convention Center.

We[2] have had the good fortune of having you as a principal speaker several times in the past, and we are[3] wondering if you would consent to speak at this year's convention. We will, of course, pay all your expenses and an[4] honorarium of $300.

We hope you will accept our invitation and speak on the subject of[5] personal investment. We are allotting one hour for this particular session.

If you will be able to[6] participate in our program this year, please let us know as soon as possible; we will then finalize our plans.[7] We sincerely hope that you will be able to join us, Dr. Weston. Sincerely yours, [156]

6 Dear Professor Stone: Recently I had the pleasure of attending a short course that you conducted on the subject[1] of employee motivation. I was very much impressed with the suggestions you offered. When I returned[2] to work, I implemented many of them immediately. The results have been both gratifying and[3] rewarding.

The morale in the office has changed dramatically in the past two weeks, and I want all the supervisors[4] in my office to learn and utilize your techniques. Would it be possible for you to come to our office[5] and present a similar course for the supervisors here? We would be willing to pay your regular fee for[6] conducting the course.

Will you please let me hear from you soon. Sincerely yours, [133]

7 To All Department Heads: Please mark next Thursday and Friday on your calendars. On those days we will have a very[1] special opportunity to attend a short course that should prove to be quite worthwhile for each of us. The course will be[2] held in our conference room on the fourth floor and will start at nine each morning. The sessions will last until five in[3] the afternoon.

The subject will be improving public relations. Dr. Lydia Mendez from Union State[4] College in New Jersey will lead the discussion. As you probably know, Dr. Mendez is a nationally[5] recognized leader in the field of public relations. She promises to share with us many new techniques that[6] have been developed recently to help improve public relations.

Please plan to attend the short course; you will be[7] glad you did. Ray Jenkins [144]

8 Dear Mr. Conway: Thank you for speaking at the Troy Publishing Association meeting last week. The members[1] of our organization have expressed their gratitude and appreciation for your taking time from your busy[2] schedule to be with us. We all want to thank you for the many fine suggestions that you made, of course.

As you[3] will remember, you asked for reactions to your presentation. Therefore, I prepared a short questionnaire that was[4] distributed to those in attendance. Ninety of the questionnaires were returned to me; they are enclosed. I am[5] also enclosing a brief summary of the reactions. I hope these comments will be of value to you as[6] you prepare other presentations.

We genuinely appreciate your time with us at our meeting, and we[7] hope that you will be able to make a similar presentation at next year's meeting. Sincerely yours, [158]

CHAPTER 16

LESSON 76

3 Ladies and Gentlemen: The Edwards Insurance Company is pleased to announce a new group life insurance plan[1] for companies located in the state of Illinois. Any company that has more than 100 employees[2] can take advantage of the great savings that we are now offering. Your organization can qualify[3] for the plan if as many as one-half of your employees wish to participate in the program.

When you purchase[4] a group life insurance policy from the Edwards Insurance Company, each of your employees will have[5] $50,000 in life insurance coverage. The policy will take effect immediately when[6] the plan is signed; no one will have to take a physical examination.

Best of all, we can provide this[7] excellent coverage for you at a cost that is only about two-thirds of what you would ordinarily expect[8] to pay.

If you would like to provide your employees with group life insurance, just call us at 555-6108.[9] We will be glad to send one of our representatives to your offices to discuss our insurance[10] plans with you. Your call will place you under no obligation, of course. Sincerely yours, [216]

4 Dear Ms. Anderson: Spring is almost here, and everyone is ready for warm weather after 4 1/2 cold,[1] snowy months.

It is wonderful to see the first flowers of spring. However, spring also brings great quantities of[2] rain to our area. Three and one-half inches of rain fell on the first day of spring last year. Before the season[3] ended, we had received more than twice the normal amount of precipitation. There was a great deal of flooding,[4] and many people lost thousands of dollars because they did not have flood insurance.

Is your home adequately[5] protected from flooding? Even if your home is not located in a floodplain, you could still suffer substantial[6] financial loss if a major flood occurred.

For only a few dollars per month, you can protect yourself from losses[7] due to flooding. Doesn't it make good sense to purchase flood insurance for your home? Put your mind at ease; call us[8] today. We will be glad to explain our company's flood insurance programs in detail. Then you can sit back and[9] enjoy spring without worrying about possible flooding. Sincerely yours, [194]

5 Dear Mr. Baker: Thank you for your order for hardware supplies from our wholesale company. We were particularly[1] happy to receive your order because it was the first time you have used the credit that you established[2] with our company 3 1/2 months ago. Enclosed are the following items:

1. A box of 1/16-inch[3] drill bits
2. A box of 3/16-inch drill bits
3. An electric drill

Unfortunately, we do not have[4] the other items that you ordered in stock at the present time. However, we should have them in the next week or[5] so. We will send them to you just as soon as they arrive at our warehouse. We will not bill you for any of the[6] other items until after the first of the month.

Thank you for your order, Mr. Baker. We are pleased to be[7] able to serve you. Sincerely yours, [147]

6 Dear Depositor: The State National Bank is happy to announce that beginning July 21 we will[1] pay 5 1/2 percent interest on the funds in your checking account.

At the end of each month, we will compute[2] your average daily balance for the month. If this figure is $400 or more, we will credit 5 1/2[3] percent interest to your account (figured on an annual basis). We are delighted to be the first[4] commercial bank in the area to give you what you deserve–interest on your checking account.

If you would like[5] to have more information about our new program, just call or stop by the bank during regular banking hours[6]–9 a.m. to 4 p.m. We will be happy to speak with you. Sincerely yours, [134]

7 Mr. Davis: On January 1 our savings bank will begin charging 14 1/2 percent interest[1] on home mortgages. As you know, this is an increase of 1 1/2 percent over our current rates. In[2] addition, we are asking that anyone wishing to obtain a home mortgage be able to make a down payment[3] of 25 percent, which is 5 percent more than our current requirement.

Will you please see that each member of your[4] department is aware of these changes. Nancy Adams [90]

LESSON 77

3 Dear Bill: Congratulations! We are all so very proud of you on your graduation from college. This represents[1] a major accomplishment in your life, and you can look back on the past four years with a great deal of personal[2] satisfaction.

I am sending you a small gift to commemorate this very special event in your life;[3] it should arrive at your home within a day or two.

Have you decided where you will be working next fall? I am[4] sure that you will have many interesting, exciting opportunities for employment. Please let me know where you[5] will be working just as soon as you are settled in your new position.

If you are in the Denver, Colorado,[6] area during the summer, I hope you will stop by my office; it will be a real pleasure to see you[7] again. Very sincerely yours, [146]

4 Dear Mr. Gates: The Jennings Supermarkets Corporation is asking for a variance in the Springfield city[1] zoning ordinance in order to construct a beautiful new supermarket on the corner of Fifth[2] Avenue and Elm Street. In order to obtain the variance, we must obtain the signatures of 20 percent[3] of the property owners within 200 feet of the site.

Your property falls into this category,[4] and we need to have your signature on the petition. Will you please sign the petition when one of our[5] representatives brings it to your home next week? By doing so you will help to assure the construction of a beautiful,[6] convenient supermarket in your neighborhood. The supermarket will make shopping easier and more[7] convenient for you and your neighbors.

Please call us at 555-8106. We will have someone come to your home[8] to obtain your signature at a time that is convenient for you.

Please help us in this way; you will be glad you[9] did! Sincerely yours, [184]

5 Dear Mr. Simmons: Thank you for writing to us about the addition you are planning for your home at[1] 8109 62d Street here in Wheeling, West Virginia. We will be very happy to submit a bid[2] on the work that you want to have done.

Before we can give you an estimate of the cost of the work, we will have[3] to visit your property to see firsthand exactly what will be involved. The actual work required can vary[4] significantly from house to house. If the basic structure is sound, we will probably be able to do[5] the work at an exceedingly low cost. If the basic structure is unsound, however, the cost could be substantially[6] higher.

One of our representatives will call you within the next week to make an appointment to come[7] to your home to speak with you. We are delighted to have the opportunity to give you an estimate on[8] the work. Sincerely yours, [164]

6 Dear Customer: Where can you make savings of 50 percent on men's, women's, and children's clothing every day? At[1] the Brown Department Store!

The Brown Department Store is your one-stop clothing center in Greenville. At no other retail[2] store in the city can you make such incredible savings on everyday clothing, on sports clothing, and on[3] formal attire.

The Brown Department Store is located at 7420 First Street. We are open from[4] 10 a.m. until 9 p.m. Monday through Saturday; we are closed all day on Sunday. If you have not visited[5] our store recently, plan to come in soon. You will be glad you did! Cordially yours, [115]

7 Dear Mary: Congratulations on your new job! We here at the Eastern Business College are all very proud of[1] you!

We knew when you enrolled in our secretarial administration program last year that you would soon have[2] a position of major responsibility. We never dreamed, however, that you would start as an executive[3] secretary to the chief executive officer of a major manufacturing company.[4] This is an accomplishment that will be hard for our current students to match.

We hope you will plan to come back to[5] Eastern Business College to tell our students all about your new position. You will always be welcome at our[6] school. Very sincerely yours, [125]

8 Dear Mr. Miller: How happy I

was when I received your letter in today's mail! It is not often that a[1] company gets such a wonderful letter telling what a good job it is doing. Usually companies hear[2] from customers by mail only when they are dissatisfied with products or services.

I am sending a copy[3] of your letter to Miss Cunningham, the head of our sporting goods department. She will be just as happy to[4] read your glowing comments as I was.

We want you to know, Mr. Miller, that we will do everything in our power[5] to continue to serve you as well as we have in the past. Such good customers deserve our best service![6] Cordially yours, [122]

9 Dear Miss White: On Tuesday, November 6, you will have the opportunity to vote for the city, county, and[1] state officials who will serve our area for the next two years.

We think it is extremely important that every[2] eligible person cast his or her ballot on Election Day. It doesn't actually matter which[3] candidates you vote for; what really matters is that you vote.

Last year only one-half of the eligible voters[4] went to the polls. This year the League of Voters is hoping that at least two-thirds of those who are eligible will[5] vote.

Do not fail to exercise one of the most valuable rights you have—the right to vote. The polls open at[6] 7 a.m. and will remain open until 8 p.m. Vote on Election Day; it is your right—and your duty![7] Yours truly, [142]

LESSON 78

3 Dear Mr. Reid: Here are some very interesting statistics concerning the Nashville General Hospital. During[1] the past year we served more than 2,000 people in our emergency room. Our staff of nationally[2] recognized surgeons performed an average of five major operations each day. In all, our hospital met the health[3] needs (major and minor) of more than 10,000 people in our community.

During the year we experienced[4] an increase in operating expenses of nearly 30 percent. However, our income remained almost[5] stable. You can easily see that we cannot continue to serve the needs of our city unless we increase[6] our income substantially.

We are soliciting funds from the general public again this year to help[7] defray the exceedingly high costs of running a hospital. This year we will try to meet a goal of[8] $1 million. We realize that this is a large sum; however, we believe that we can reach the goal.

Because you have[9] contributed generously in the past, we know that you understand the importance of maintaining a first-class[10] medical facility in our community. Won't you please sign the enclosed pledge card and return it to[11] us in the envelope that is provided. You will be making a wise investment in the future of our city[12]—and in your own future as well. Yours truly, [249]

4 Dear Mr. and Mrs. Nottingham: The International Travel Agency is sponsoring a special tour[1] to Europe for antique dealers. The tour will include stops in England, Scotland, and Wales. The tour will commence in Houston[2] on June 3; we will then fly to London. We will conclude the tour by flying back to Houston from Wales on July[3] 3. We will visit not only the major cities in each country but small towns and villages as well.

Our[4] group will travel together most of the time. However, there will be four 2-day side trips that will be especially[5] planned for each individual person. You will have ample time at each stop to buy those special items that[6] you will want to ship back to the United States to sell in your antique shop.

We are limiting our group to[7] 25 people this year. The reason is that we want to be able to stay in country inns that cannot[8] accommodate large groups. Last year we had to turn away a number of people who wanted to go on the tour because[9] they submitted their applications too late. Don't delay; make your reservations today. You will have a[10] wonderful time, and you will probably find many unusual antiques for your store. Cordially yours, [218]

5 Dear Mr. Carson: As attorney for the Mason Department Store, I have the responsibility of[1] advising the company on any matters that involve the law. In yesterday's mail I received a letter from[2] Miss Jane Kelley, credit manager of the store. Miss Kelley informed me that you signed a binding contract with the[3] store on January 21 to pay for furniture that you purchased. The total amount was $3,000,[4] and you made two $100 payments. The first payment was made in February; the second payment[5] was made in March. Since that time, however, you have not made any further payments.

I am sure you realize that[6] your action is a breach of contract. The Mason Department Store does not necessarily wish to bring charges[7] against you, but if you do not bring your account up to date, I must advise them that we have no other alternative.[8]

If you do not submit a check for $1,000 by January 15 to bring your account[9] into balance, I will be forced to initiate a lawsuit against you. As I am sure I need not tell you,[10] this could make obtaining credit at other retail establishments extremely difficult.

Do yourself and the[11] Mason Department Store a favor, Mr. Carson. Place your check in the mail before the 15th. Yours truly, [239]

6 Dear Mr. Lang: Some insurance companies send representatives to knock on doors to try to sell their policies.[1] Others send dozens of pieces of mail. Still others make repeated telephone calls.

We here at the National[2] Insurance Company do not do any of these things. We place one–and only one–letter in the mail along[3] with a brochure that explains our services. We do not use bulk mail; every letter that we send is a[4] personal one. We feel that people recognize the need for insurance and that all we should do is make our services[5] known to them. The choice about which insurance company to choose is theirs; it is not ours.

We hope you will read[6] the enclosed brochure, Mr. Lang. It explains each of our insurance programs in detail. After you have had an[7] opportunity to study the brochure, we will be happy to answer any questions you may have. You may[8] call us at 555-6161, or you may return the enclosed card. We will ask one of our well-trained,[9] experienced representatives to call you or to visit you–whichever you specify. However, we will[10] do nothing unless we hear from you.

Isn't this the logical, sensible approach to purchasing insurance?[11] If you think it is, just contact us; we will be glad to hear from you. Sincerely yours, [235]

LESSON 79

Office-Style Dictation

1 *(As dictated)* Dear Mr. Taylor: I am sure you realize that your bill for the supplies (make that *hardware and plumbing supplies*) that you bought in our store several months ago (change that to *on Friday, January 20,*) is now past due. Although we have sent you three reminders, you have not sent us your payment or even acknowledged receiving the statements.

Please (let's make that *Will you please*) take a moment right now to either send us your check for $200 in full payment or at least let us know what the problem is.

We will be looking for a letter from you by return mail. Sincerely yours,

1 *(As it would be transcribed)* Dear Mr. Taylor: I am sure you realize that your bill for the hardware and plumbing supplies that you bought in our[1] store on Friday, January 20, is now past due. Although we have sent you three reminders, you have not sent[2] us your payment or even acknowledged receiving the statements.

Will you please take a moment right now to either[3] send us your check for $200 in full payment or at least let us know what the problem is.

We will be[4] looking for a letter from you by return mail. Sincerely yours, [92]

3 To All Employees: As you know, we are installing eight new elevators in our office building at the present[1] time. These new automatic elevators will replace the slow, old-fashioned ones that we have used since our building[2] was constructed in 1950.

Unfortunately, we will all experience some delays in getting[3] to and from our offices while the new elevators are being installed. There will be only one or two[4] elevators in service most of the time from now until August 1, when all the new elevators should be working.[5]

We hope that each of you will be patient with us during these trying times and that you will do everything[6] possible to minimize the inconvenience that we will all experience. Bill Adams [136]

4 Dear Voters: For the past few months there has been a great deal of controversy concerning the construction of a[1] proposed shopping center in suburban Springfield. Those who want the shopping center built contend that it would bring hundreds[2] of new jobs to the area. However, those who do not want the center constructed say that it would take[3] a great deal of business away from the older, established commercial centers in the area.

It is the[4] feeling of the members of the Chamber of Commerce that the center would be a very good thing for the city[5] and the surrounding areas. The commercial centers in the vicinity have already experienced[6] a serious decline in business. Not allowing the shopping center to be constructed would not bring business[7] back to these areas. Permitting the center to be built would add significantly to the tax base of the[8] county.

We hope you agree with us that the construction of the new center is vital to our area and that[9] you will ask your friends and neighbors to send letters to the county commissioners soliciting their support in[10] this matter. Yours truly, [204]

5 Dear Miss White: I just received the manuscript for the article that you wrote for the March 14 issue of *Business*[1] *Day*. Congratulations; you have done an excellent job! I am exceedingly happy with the article;[2] it covers the topic of women in business very well indeed. I am recommending that the article[3] be used without major changes–just minor deletions or additions.

I am forwarding the manuscript to[4] Ms. Betty Green, who is responsible for editing our publications. I am sure you will be hearing from[5] Ms. Green in the next few days.

We look forward to receiving more manuscripts from you in the future, Miss White.[6] Sincerely yours, [122]

6 Dear Mr. Edwards: Did you know that you have a new office supply shop right in your own neighborhood? Yes, just this[1] week the Western Office Supply Company opened its doors for the first time. We are located at 896[2] East 23 Street, which is only a few blocks away from your office building.

We are very glad to be[3] able to serve the Madison, Wisconsin, area, and we want to invite you to come to our store to see[4] the large selection of office supplies that we have on our shelves. We have a complete line of every type of bond[5] paper manufactured today. In addition, we have hundreds of other items that are needed to run modern[6] offices with efficiency.

Stop by anytime between nine in the morning and six in the afternoon.[7] We will be more than happy to serve you. Sincerely yours, [150]

7 Miss Kelly: Several weeks ago, I received a copy of the memorandum that you mailed to each of the[1] sales representatives in our organization. What a good job you did!

Although you had to tell our[2] representatives that they would be receiving their commissions more than two months late this year, I am sure each one of them[3] understands the reasons for the delay. This type of memorandum is quite difficult to compose, and bad news[4] is never greeted warmly. However, we have not had a negative comment to this date.

You may be sure, Miss[5] Kelly, that we will be calling on you to handle other difficult, challenging jobs in the future. Robert[6] Martin [121]

8 Mr. Martin: Thanks so much for your comments about the memorandum I mailed to each of the sales representatives[1] in our organization. You are quite right; it is not easy to *compose** a memorandum containing[2] bad news. I must admit that it took me several hours to write it.

I am very happy that you would like[3] me to handle other difficult jobs for you in the future. Whenever you need any *assistance*†, just let[4] me know. Nancy Kelly [84]

Also correct:

*write

†help

LESSON 80

3 Dear Professor Sloan: Today is the day of the computer in education. Many colleges now have 5,[1] 10, or even 20 small computers in their classes for their students to use. These computers are utilized[2] to teach everything from math to English grammar and from basic spelling to reading.

The National Computer[3] Company can supply you with inexpensive, small computers for the students in your college. In addition,[4] we can supply you with the software that you will need to make the computer a truly educational tool.[5]

Would you like to have more information about small computers that are designed for educational purposes,[6] Professor Sloan? If you would, just call Mr. Max Dempsey, our representative in your area. He will[7] be glad to come to your office to tell you all about the advantages computers offer to educators.[8] Cordially yours, [164]

4 Dear Mr. Cunningham: Are you certain that you are wearing the right clothing when you leave for the office in the[1] morning? Are you sure that you have chosen the correct suit to wear to a special occasion after six in the[2] evening?

If you would like to feel more confident about the clothes that you purchase, come to the Hamilton Men's Store,[3] which is located at 8160 Main Street here in Providence, Rhode Island. When you shop at the Hamilton[4] Men's Store, you will receive the expert advice of people who have been in the men's clothing business for more than[5] ten years. They know what clothes to recommend for every occasion, and they can recommend the styles that are[6] particularly good for you.

What does this valuable service cost? It costs nothing! It is free when you come to visit[7] our shop.

Come in soon and talk with our well-trained, experienced people; you will be glad you did. Sincerely yours, [159]

5 Dear Mr. Paul: The Jenkins Hardware Shop, which has been in business in Detroit since July 1, 1950, will[1] be closing its doors for the last time in only a few weeks.

We have decided that it is time to retire and[2] catch up on the swimming, boating, and golfing that we have been postponing for so many years.

Before we close our[3] doors, however, we want to say thank you to our loyal friends and customers who have supported us over the[4] years. We want to do so by offering you very special prices on every item in our store.

During the[5] week of February 5, we will be offering our regular customers bargains that will be hard to pass[6] by. Every item in our store will be on sale at one-half the original price. All you need do to take[7] advantage of these great savings is present this letter to one of our clerks when you make a purchase. The sale will not[8] be open to the public until after our regular customers have had a full week to make any[9] purchases they wish.

We think this is a particularly appropriate way of saying thanks for your patronage over[10] the years; we hope you will agree. Cordially yours, [210]

6 Dear Mr. Wilson: Yesterday I received the attached letter from a disgruntled customer. The letter states[1] in part: "I was in your store recently and purchased several very expensive items. When I returned to[2] my home, I found that the items were not of the quality that I expected. I would like a full refund."

We[3] occasionally receive similar letters from customers; however, this letter is special in two ways:[4]

1. The person has been a loyal customer of ours for more than ten years.
2. The goods were purchased more than two[5] months ago.

We ordinarily do not accept goods for a full refund if they are not returned within a[6] week's time. In this case, however, it seems that we should make an exception. However, I will leave the matter[7] entirely in your hands. Please advise me of the action you plan to take. Martin Moses [155]

APPENDIX

RECALL DRILLS

Joined Word Endings

1 Treatment, alignment, supplement, amusement, compliment, experiment.

2 Nation, termination, station, operation, inflation, relation, caution, portion, section, promotion.

3 Credential, confidential, essential, commercial, socially.

4 Greatly, namely, nicely, mainly, nearly, highly, only, properly, surely, mostly.

5 Readily, speedily, easily, hastily, necessarily, family.

6 Careful, thoughtful, delightful, mindful, usefulness, awful, helpful, powerful, respectful, faithful.

7 Dependable, reliable, profitable, table, troubled.

8 Gather, gathered, together, rather, either, leather, bother, bothered, neither, mother.

9 Actual, actually, gradual, schedule, annual, equally.

10 Furniture, picture, nature, stature, captured, miniature, failure, natural, feature.

11 Yourself, myself, itself, himself, herself, themselves, ourselves, yourselves.

12 Port, sport, import, report, deportment.

13 Contain, retain, certain, container, contained.

14 Efficient, sufficient, deficient, efficiency, deficiency, proficiency.

Disjoined Word Endings

15 Childhood, motherhood, neighborhood, brotherhood.

16 Forward, backward, onward, afterward, rewarded.

17 Relationship, steamship, authorship, professorship, championship.

18 Radical, technical, political, article, chemically, periodically, logically, practically.

19 Congratulate, regulate, stipulates, tabulated, congratulation, regulation, regulations, stipulations.

20 Willingly, exceedingly, knowingly, surprisingly, grudgingly.

21 Readings, mornings, sidings, dressings, savings, drawings, sayings, blessings, feelings, servings.

22 Program, telegram, telegrams, diagrams.

23 Notification, modification, specifications, classifications, ratification.

24 Personality, ability, reliability, facilities, utility, generalities, locality.

25 Faculty, penalty, casualty, loyalty.

26 Authority, sincerity, majority, minority, clarity, sorority, charity, seniority.

Joined Word Beginnings

27 Permit, perform, perfect, pertain, persist, purchase, pursue, pursued, purple, purse.

28 Employ, empower, embarrass, embody, empire, emphatic, embrace, emphasis, emphasize.

29 Impress, impression, imply, impossible, impair, impel, imbue, impact, imperfect.

30 Increase, intend, income, inform, inconsistent, indeed, inference, inferior, insane, inscribe.

31 Enlarge, enforce, enlist, encourage, enjoy, enrich, encounter, encircle, enrage.
32 Unkind, unwritten, unwilling, unsuccessful, undo, unpleasant, untie, unpopular.
33 Refer, resign, receive, reform, reorganize.
34 Beneath, believe, belong, before, became.
35 Delay, deliver, deserve, diligent.
36 Dismiss, disappoint, discover, discuss, despite.
37 Mistake, misquote, misspell, misstate, misunderstand, misapplied, mistrust.
38 Explain, excite, extend, excuse, express, exit.
39 Comprise, comfort, comply, completed, compete.
40 Condition, consult, continue, confident, convey, confess.
41 Submit, substantiate, subdivide, sublease, suburban.
42 Almost, also, already, although, alteration.
43 Forget, forceful, performed, forecast, foreman.
44 Furnish, furnished, furnishings, furniture, furnace, further, furtive.
45 Turn, turned, term, attorney, determine, eastern.
46 Ultimate, ulterior, adult, culture, result.

Disjoined Word Beginnings

47 Interested, internal, interview, intercept, introduce, entrance, entrances, introduction, enterprise, entertain, entered.
48 Electricity, electrician, electrical, electric wire, electric fan, electric light, electric motor, electrode.
49 Supervise, supervision, supervisor, superhuman, superb, superior.
50 Circumstance, circumstances, circumstantial, circumvent, circumspect.
51 Selfish, self-made, self-defense, self-respect, self-conscious, self-assured.
52 Transit, transfer, transact, transplant, translation.
53 Understand, undertake, undergo, underpaid, undermine, understate, underline, underscore, understood, undercover.
54 Overcome, overdue, overhead, overture, overpay, oversee, overdraw, overgrow, overlook, overnight, oversight.

Key to Chart on Page 448

Brief Forms of Gregg Shorthand in Alphabetical Order

1 A-an, about, acknowledge, advantage, advertise, after, am.
2 And, any, are-our-hour, be-by, business, but, can.
3 Character, characters, circular, company, correspond-correspondence, corresponded, could.
4 Difficult, doctor, enclose, envelope, every-ever, executive, experience.
5 For, from, general, gentlemen, glad, good, govern.
6 Government, have, I, idea, immediate, important-importance, in-not.

7 Is-his, it-at, manufacture, morning, Mr., Mrs., Ms.
8 Never, newspaper, next, object, objected, of, one (won).
9 Opinion, opportunity, order, ordinary, organize, out, over.
10 Part, particular, present, probable, progress, public, publish-publication.
11 Quantity, question, recognize, regard, regular, request, responsible.
12 Satisfy-satisfactory, send, several, short, should, soon, speak.
13 State, street, subject, success, suggest, than, thank.
14 That, the, them, there (their), they, thing-think, this.
15 Throughout, time, under, usual, value, very, was.
16 Were, what, when, where, which, will-well, wish.
17 With, work, world, worth, would, yesterday, you-your.